ROUGH GUIDES

T0082326

POCKET **ROUGH GUIDE**
LAS VEGAS

updated by
PAUL STAFFORD

LONGHORN
CASINO · HOTEL

HOT SEATS
SAT - THURS 10AM - 10PM
EVERY SPIN A GUARANTEED WIN!
2X POINTS ON FRIDAY

16 oz. Porterhouse
$8.99
4 p.m. - Midnight

CONTENTS

LAS VEGAS

A dazzling oasis where about forty million people a year escape the everyday, Las Vegas has made a fine art of indulging its visitors' every appetite. From its ever-changing architecture to cascading chocolate fountains, adrenaline-pumping zip lines and jaw-dropping stage shows, everything is built to thrill; as soon as the novelty wears off, it's blown up and replaced with something bigger and better. The city of excess is home to some of the largest hotels in the world – and that's pretty much all – but it's these extraordinary creations everyone comes to see.

Fremont Street Experience

Best places to get a view of the Strip

Although towering hotel blocks jostle for position along the Strip, there are surprisingly few places that offer non-guests a panoramic view of the whole thing. Possibilities include the summit of the Stratosphere (but that's at the northern edge of what's considered to be the Strip), and the Voodoo Rooftop Nightclub at the Rio, off to one side. So the winner is – the observation platform at the top of Paris's Eiffel Tower (see page 49), perfectly poised to look north and south along the Strip's busiest stretch, as well as west, and down, to the fountains of Bellagio.

Each hotel is a neighbourhood in its own right, measuring as much as a mile end to end; crammed full of state-of-the-art clubs, restaurants, spas and pools; and centring on what makes the whole thing possible – an action-packed casino where tourists and tycoons alike are gripped by the roll of the dice and the turn of the card.

Even if its entire urban area covers 136 square miles, most visitors see no more of Las Vegas than two short, and very different, linear stretches. Downtown, the original centre, now amounts to four brief (roofed-over) blocks of Fremont Street, while the Strip begins a couple of miles south, just beyond the city limits, and runs for five miles southwest. It's the Strip where the real action is, a visual feast where each mega-casino vies to outdo the next with some outlandish theme, be it an Egyptian pyramid (*Luxor*), a Roman extravaganza (*Caesars Palace*), a fairytale castle (*Excalibur*) or a European city (*Paris* and the *Venetian*).

In 1940, Las Vegas was home to just eight thousand people. It owes its extraordinary growth to its constant willingness to adapt; far from remaining kitsch and old-fashioned, it's forever reinventing itself. Entrepreneurs race to spot the latest shift in who has the money and what they want to spend it on. A few years ago the casinos realized that gamblers were happy to pay premium prices for good food, and top chefs now run gourmet restaurants in venues like *Bellagio* and the *Cosmopolitan*. More recently, demand from younger visitors has prompted casinos like *Wynn Las Vegas* and *MGM Grand* to open high-tech nightclubs to match those of Miami and LA.

The reputation Las Vegas still enjoys, of being a quasi-legal adult playground where (almost) anything goes, dates back to its early years when most of its first generation of luxury resorts were cut-throat rivals controlled by the Mob. In those days illegal profits could easily be "skimmed" off and respectable investors steered clear. Then, as now, visitors loved to imagine that they were rubbing shoulders with gangsters. Standing well back from the Strip, each casino was a labyrinth in which it was all but impossible to find an exit. During the 1980s, however, visitors started to explore on foot; mogul Steve Wynn cashed in by placing a flame-spouting volcano outside his new Mirage mega-resort. As the casinos competed to lure in pedestrians, they filled in the daunting distances from the sidewalk, and between casinos.

With Las Vegas booming in the 1990s, gaming corporations bought up first individual casinos, and then each other. The Strip today is dominated by just two colossal conglomerates – MGM Resorts

When to visit

Visitors flock to Las Vegas throughout the year, however the climate varies enormously. In July and August, the average daytime high exceeds 100°F (38°C), while in winter the thermometer regularly drops below freezing. Hotel swimming pools generally open between April and September only.
It's which day you visit that you should really take into account; accommodation can easily cost twice as much on Friday and Saturday as during the rest of the week.

and Caesars Entertainment. Once you own the casino next door, there's no reason to make each a virtual prison. The Strip has therefore opened out, so that much of its central portion now consists of open-air terraces and pavilions housing bars and restaurants. Strolling its four miles is like entering a parallel universe.

The city may have tamed its setting, but the magnificent wildernesses of the American West still lie on its doorstep. Dramatic parks like Red Rock Canyon and the Valley of Fire are just a short drive away, or you can fly to the Grand Canyon, and Utah's glorious Zion National Park makes a wonderful overnight getaway.

Valley of Fire

Where to...

Shop

Shopping now ranks among the principal reasons that people visit Las Vegas. **Downtown** is all but devoid of shops, however, and while the workaday city has its fair share of malls, tourists do almost all of their shopping on **the Strip** itself. Their prime destination is the amazing **Forum** at Caesars Palace, followed by the **Grand Canal Shoppes** at the Venetian and **Miracle Mile** at Planet Hollywood. Stand-alone malls include **Fashion Show** opposite Wynn Las Vegas, useful for everyday purchases, and high-end **Crystals** in CityCenter.

OUR FAVOURITES: Town Square, see page 32. Miracle Mile Shops, see page 56. Grand Canal Shoppes, see page 70.

Eat

Las Vegas used to be a byword for bad food, with just the occasional mobster-dominated steakhouse or Italian restaurant to relieve the monotony of the pile-'em-high **buffets**. Those days have long gone. Every major **Strip casino** now holds half a dozen or more high-quality restaurants, many run by top chefs from all over the world. Prices have soared, to a typical minimum spend of $75 per head at big-name places, but so too have standards, and you could eat a great meal in a different restaurant every night at any of the big casinos.

OUR FAVOURITES: Bacchanal Buffet at Caesars Palace, see page 56. Crossroads Kitchen, Resorts World, see page 72. Bouchon at the Venetian, see page 71.

Drink

Every Las Vegas casino offers free drinks to gamblers. Sit at a slot machine or gaming table, and a cocktail waiter will find you and take your order (tips are expected). In addition, the casinos feature all kinds of bars and lounges. Along the Strip, bars tend to be themed, as with the Irish pubs of **New York–New York** or the flamboyant lounges of **Caesars Palace**; downtown they're a bit more rough-and-ready. Note that the legal drinking age is 21 – you must carry ID to prove it.

OUR FAVOURITES: Vanderpump Cocktail Garden, see page 58. Evel Pie, see page 85. Double Down Saloon, see page 93.

Go out

The Strip is once more riding high as the entertainment epicentre of the world. While Elvis may have left the building, headliners like **David Copperfield** and **Celine Dion** attract thousands of big-spending fans night after night. Meanwhile the old-style feathers-and-sequins revues have been supplanted by a stream of lavish shows by **Cirque du Soleil** and the likes of the postmodern **Blue Man Group**. A new generation of visitors has been responsible for the dramatic growth in the city's clubbing scene. Casinos like the **Cosmopolitan**, the **Palms** and **Wynn Las Vegas** now boast some of the world's most spectacular – and expensive – nightclubs and ultra-lounges.

OUR FAVOURITES: The Colosseum, see page 59. "O" by Cirque du Soleil, see page 47. Terry Fator, see page 37.

Las Vegas at a glance

The rest of the city page 86.
Real people live real lives in Las Vegas's outlying residential districts, but for visitors the major landmarks are yet more casinos, with standouts including the Rio, the Palms and the Virgin Hotels Las Vegas.

The North Strip page 62.
Two deadly rival mega-complexes, the Venetian/Palazzo and Wynn Las Vegas/Encore lock horns at the northern end of the Strip. The area beyond them is rebounding, with sleek new casinos filling lots that were emptied of their veteran casinos during the Great Recession.

CityCenter and around page 38.
The Strip's first separate "neighbourhood", unveiled by MGM Resorts in 2009 and centring on the modernist Aria, also includes Bellagio, as well as an unwanted interloper, the Cosmopolitan.

The South Strip page 24.
With their playful architecture and varied attractions, the high-profile, MGM-owned casinos at the southern end of the Strip – Mandalay Bay, Luxor, Excalibur, New York–New York and the MGM Grand – are hugely popular with younger visitors.

Downtown Las Vegas page 78.
The few blocks where it all began
have bounced back in recent years,
with the unique Fremont Street
Experience and the Mob Museum
drawing the crowds.

N

The Central Strip page 48.
The long-standing heart of the Strip,
which includes veterans like the Flamingo
and Caesars Palace as well as the newer
Paris, belongs entirely to Caesars
Entertainment, and has become its most
pedestrian-friendly segment.

▷ **The deserts** page 96.
For a taste of Nevada's desert scenery,
venture twenty miles west of Las Vegas
to Red Rock Canyon. Wonders further
afield include Arizona's Grand Canyon
and Utah's Zion Canyon.

0	kilometres	2
0	mile	1

15 Things not to miss

It's not possible to see everything that Las Vegas has to offer in one trip – and we don't suggest you try. What follows is a selective taste of the highlights, from its most opulent casinos to the dramatic scenery of the deserts.

> The Forum Shops
See page 56
America's most profitable shopping mall, stuffed inside the faux-Roman pomp of Caesars Palace – though the price tags are real enough.

< Grand Canyon South Rim
See page 100
Seeing Arizona's world-famous wonder makes a fabulous weekend road trip, but you can also fly there and back in a day.

∨ The Venetian
See page 63
Festooned with dazzling frescoes and echoing to the song of costumed gondoliers, the opulent Venetian is loved by kids, clubbers and culture vultures alike.

< **Zion National Park**
See page 100
You can drive to Utah's magnificent red-rock park in little more than two hours to enjoy dramatic scenery and breathtaking hikes.

∨ **Dig This!**
See page 87
If you've always wanted to drive a bulldozer, or play basketball using a giant digger, this is where your dreams come true.

THINGS NOT TO MISS

∧ **Kà**
See page 36
For sheer spectacle and breathtaking stunts, see the most jaw-dropping Cirque show in town.

< **The Strat Thrill Rides**
See page 69
The craziest thrill rides of all – spin off the Strat strapped to a lurching bench or simply jump off the edge.

∧ **Red Rock Canyon**
See page 96
Las Vegas's great escape;
hike and bike amid stunning
sandstone peaks just twenty
miles from the Strip.

∨ **Bellagio**
See page 42
Las Vegas at its most luxurious,
an Italianate marble extravaganza
with its own eight-acre lake.

∧ The Neon Museum
See page 81
A charming, unpolished look at a Vegas icon: the neon sign. Unsurprisingly, it's most atmospheric after dark.

‹ Titanic: The Artifact Exhibition
See page 27
The world's only permanent display of Titanic artefacts, including a huge and very eerie chunk of the ship herself, upstairs in the Luxor pyramid.

< **Blue Man Group**
See page 36
A bizarre but compelling blend of performance art, slapstick and high-octane rock.

∨ **Hoover Dam**
See page 96
A mighty wall of concrete holding back the Colorado River – the architectural showpiece that made Las Vegas possible.

THINGS NOT TO MISS

Day One in Las Vegas

🍴 **Bellagio Patisserie, Bellagio**. See page 44. Head to the back of Bellagio to enjoy a morning pick-me-up of pastries, omelettes and freshly brewed coffee.

The Conservatory, Bellagio. See page 43. Part greenhouse, part camp and colourful fantasyland, Bellagio's indoor flower show must be seen to be believed.

Eiffel Tower Experience. See page 49. Ride into the skies atop Las Vegas's own miniature version of Paris and look down on the rest of the Strip.

The Conservatory, Bellagio

🍴 **Lunch**. See page 58. Enjoy a quintessentially French bistro meal, with a ringside seat on the Strip, at *Mon Ami Gabi* in Paris.

The Forum Shops. See page 56. Marble statues, fountains and a false sky that cycles hourly between day and night; is it ancient Rome or simply Caesars Palace?

Grand Canal Shoppes. See page 70. Operatic gondoliers ply the waters of the Grand Canal, serenading shoppers perusing the Venetian's upstairs, upmarket mall.

Entrance to The Forum Shops

🍴 **Dinner**. See page 73. Pan-Asian food and lush red decor at *Wazuzu* in Wynn Las Vegas combine to offer a memorable dining experience.

Mystère, TI. See page 76. The original show from Las Vegas favourites, Cirque du Soleil, is still going strong.

Omnia, Caesars Palace. See page 60. Experience Las Vegas's new breed of breathtaking clubs at Caesars' showpiece indoor-outdoor *Omnia*.

Omnia

Day Two in Las Vegas

🍴 **Il Fornaio, New York–New York.** See page 33. This New York-style Italian bakery is the perfect place to grab breakfast.

The Big Apple Coaster, New York–New York. See page 30. Let's shake things up – loop around the Manhattan skyline in a little yellow cab, upside down, at 70mph.

Excalibur. See page 27. If things haven't been kitsch enough yet, visit this bizarre Arthurian castle-casino.

Luxor. See page 25. Enter an Egyptian pyramid through the paws of the Sphinx to see artefacts recovered from the Titanic.

Shark Reef, Mandalay Bay. See page 25. Watch crocodiles and sharks swim amid the ruins of a Maya temple.

🍴 **Lunch.** See page 32. Break for a Mexican meal beside Mandalay Bay's wave pool, at the *Border Grill*.

Hunger Games The Exhibition, MGM Grand. See page 31. Channel your inner Katniss Everdeen at the digital archery range.

Art collection, CityCenter. See page 38. The sleek, modernist CityCenter district holds a surprising array of contemporary sculptures from the likes of Maya Lin, Henry Moore and Antony Gormley.

The Shops at Crystals. See page 44. Las Vegas's priciest mall has a flamboyant interior that's well worth seeing.

🍴 **Dinner.** See page 46. Dine on superb "new Italian" food in *Scarpetta*, overlooking Bellagio's famous fountains.

Donny Osmond. See page 60. See the pop icon deliver a glittering song-and-dance show in the finest Las Vegas tradition.

Excalibur

Luxor

Shark Reef

ITINERARIES

Classic Las Vegas

For those who yearn for the Rat Pack-ruled Strip, corporate-owned Las Vegas can feel too tasteful for comfort. But vestiges of the old times survive, if you know where to look.

Flamingo Las Vegas. See page 54. Okay, so the Flamingo these days is more sequins than Siegel, but the original Strip resort still packs plenty of classic kitsch, including its trademark pink flamingos.

Caesars Palace. See page 51. With its half-naked centurions and Cleopatras, Caesars is where the Strip first veered towards full-on fantasy fifty years ago – and it hasn't let up since.

🍽 **Lunch**. See page 83. The all-you-can-eat buffet is one tradition Las Vegas will never let go; prices have risen on the Strip, but head downtown and you'll find amazing value, at the *Garden Court buffet*, for example.

The Mob Museum. See page 81. There's no better place to learn the seedy story of Las Vegas's shady past than at this gripping, gruesome museum downtown.

El Cortez. See page 80. For the true Las Vegas experience, gamble in downtown's least-changed casino, with its hard-bitten characters and rock-bottom odds.

Fremont Street Experience. See page 78. All bright lights and flashing neon, downtown's must-see block-spanning canopy is pure old-fashioned spectacle.

🍽 **Dinner**. See page 83. *Oscar's Steakhouse*, belonging to larger-than-life former mayor Oscar Goodman, oozes unabashed love for downtown's long-lost heyday.

Peppermill Fireside Lounge. See page 74. Round things off with a martini nightcap in this flamboyant round-the-clock Stripside relic.

Caesars Palace

Dynamite at the Mob Museum

Fremont Street Experience

Budget Las Vegas

While Las Vegas is not the budget destination it used to be, it's still possible to visit on the cheap if you play your cards right (better still, don't play cards at all...).

Excalibur. See page 27. Wake up in your Royal Tower room at Excalibur – they're the Strip's best value.

Free monorails. See page 118. Hop on the free monorail system to see Luxor and Mandalay Bay.

The Deuce. See page 117. Ride the Deuce bus north from Mandalay Bay and enjoy the Strip in all its glory.

The Midway. See page 68. Stop off at Circus Circus to watch free circus performances on the Midway stage.

Lunch. See page 71. Stick around at Circus Circus to sample its buffet of comfort food, from fat burritos to Asian mainstays. Open Friday to Monday, it's by far the cheapest buffet on the Strip.

Mac King. See page 61. Cross the Strip to Harrah's to enjoy the best-value show in town – the clownish, endearing Mac King and his family-fun comedy magic.

Big Elvis. See page 60. Simply stay in Harrah's and head for the no-cover Piano Bar, where the hunka-hunka love that is Pete Vallee keeps on burning all afternoon.

Lake of Dreams. See page 67. Once darkness falls, take your place on Wynn's lake level patio and watch the impressive free light, puppetry and water show.

Dinner. See page 72. Many meals come in at under $20 at the *Grand Lux Cafe*, a great-value place to fill yourself up.

Bellagio Fountains. See page 43. The mesmerizing jets of this free water ballet make a suitably soothing end to the day.

Monorail

The Deuce

The Bellagio Fountains

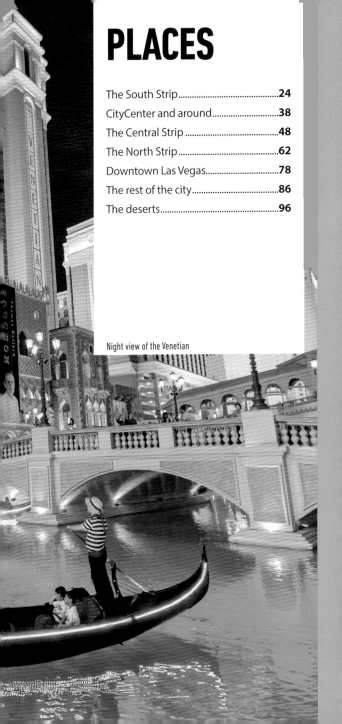

PLACES

Night view of the Venetian

The South Strip

For eight decades huge casinos have pushed ever further south along Las Vegas Boulevard, and what constitutes the South Strip has been repeatedly redefined. One thing has remained constant, however: entrepreneurs love to build lavish, eye-catching properties here because they're the first to be seen by drivers arriving from southern California. The current generation thus includes a scale model of Manhattan, New York–New York; Leo the Lion and the vast MGM Grand; fantasy castle Excalibur; an Egyptian pyramid and Sphinx, Luxor; and what's currently the true start of the Strip, gleaming tropical paradise Mandalay Bay. Thanks to successive buyouts and mergers, all five are now owned by MGM Resorts and run as a cohesive unit. The exception, ageing Tropicana, not surprisingly struggles to keep up.

Mandalay Bay

MAP P.26, POCKET MAP B7
3950 Las Vegas Blvd S
Ⓦ mandalaybay.com.

The southernmost mega-casino on the Strip, **Mandalay Bay**, consists of two golden skyscrapers that tower over a sprawling complex covering a greater area than any other single property in Las Vegas. Linked to Luxor (see page 25) and Excalibur (see page 27) by a stand-alone outdoor **monorail** (also called the tram) as well as indoor walkways, it belongs to the same owners, MGM Resorts. It was built in 1999 to provide a more sophisticated alternative to what were then its more overtly child-oriented neighbours, and apart from the **Shark Reef** aquarium (see page 25) offers little to lure in casual sightseers.

Beyond a certain vague tropical theming, there's no significance to the name "Mandalay". Instead Mandalay Bay's strongest selling point is its nightlife, with a high-end array of restaurants, beach clubs and bars – such as *Foundation Room* (see page 36),

and music venues, including the prestigious *House of Blues* (see page 36), plus the self-explanatory Cirque show, *Michael Jackson One*. To keep its young, affluent guests on site during the day as well, there's also an impressively landscaped network of pools and artificial beaches that includes a wave pool and the "toptional" (i.e. optionally topless) **Moorea Beach Club**.

Being further south of the Strip's centre of gravity than most would choose to walk, Mandalay Bay can feel a little stranded. Forced to work hard to attract and keep visitors, however, it continues to prosper. Inevitably, some of its restaurants have lost their original buzz, while the Mandalay Place mall has little to lure shoppers based elsewhere. For a night out, though, or a weekend in a self-contained luxury resort, Mandalay Bay can still match the best Las Vegas has to offer.

Incidentally, the *Four Seasons* hotel is right here too – its rooms occupy the top five floors of Mandalay Bay's original tower.

Shark Reef

MAP P.26, POCKET MAP B8
Mandalay Bay, 3950 Las Vegas Blvd
Ⓦ sharkreef.com. Charge.

In keeping with Las Vegas's emphasis on immediate thrills, the **Shark Reef** aquarium focuses almost exclusively on dangerous marine predators, prowling through tanks designed to resemble a decaying ancient temple that's sinking into the sea. The species on show – largely chosen for their scary teeth and deadly stings – include giant crocodiles and Komodo dragons, as well, of course, as enormous sharks. Separate eerily illuminated cylindrical tanks are filled with menacing-looking jellyfish. Add-on tickets offer hands-on (so to speak) shark or stingray feedings.

Shark Reef is located right at the back of Mandalay Bay; to reach it, you have to walk along several hundred yards of internal corridors, beyond the two convention centres.

Luxor

MAP P.26, POCKET MAP B6
3900 Las Vegas Blvd S Ⓦ luxor.com.

The Luxor Pyramid

The huge **Luxor** pyramid, with its sloping, monolithic walls of black shiny glass, was built in 1993 as the follow-up to the much more fanciful Excalibur (see page 27) next door. Originally it was filled to bursting with ancient Egyptian motifs, including not only a replica of King Tut's tomb but even an indoor River Nile. Then, when Las Vegas (and owners MGM Resorts in particular) decided to gear itself less towards kids and more towards adults, much of Luxor's archaeological theming was stripped away. Nothing can mask the fact that it's a colossal pyramid, though, and Luxor today seems to be in an odd sort of limbo, embarrassed about its Egyptian past but unable to find an alternative identity.

Visitors who venture this far down the Strip – especially those arriving on the **Mandalay Bay–Excalibur Tram** – still congregate outside to take photos of the enormous Sphinx that straddles the main driveway. Immediately inside the main doors, there's also a re-creation of the facade of the Egyptian temple of Abu Simbel.

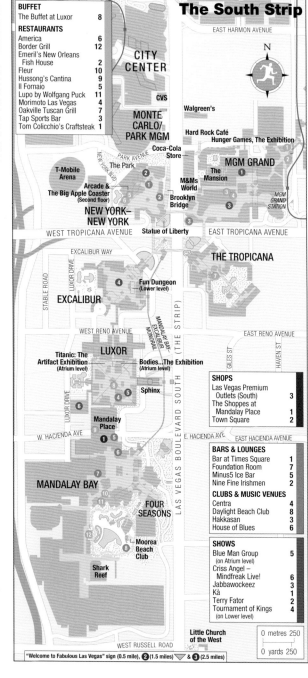

The South Strip

BUFFET
The Buffet at Luxor ... 8

RESTAURANTS
America ... 6
Border Grill ... 12
Emeril's New Orleans
  Fish House ... 2
Fleur ... 10
Hussong's Cantina ... 9
Il Fornaio ... 5
Lupo by Wolfgang Puck ... 11
Morimoto Las Vegas ... 4
Oakville Tuscan Grill ... 7
Tap Sports Bar ... 3
Tom Colicchio's Craftsteak ... 1

EAST HARMON AVENUE

N

CITY CENTER

CVS

Walgreen's

MONTE CARLO/PARK MGM

Hard Rock Café

Hunger Games, The Exhibition

Coca-Cola Store

MGM GRAND

PARK AVENUE

The Park

T-Mobile Arena

M&Ms World

The Mansion

THE MANSION

Arcade & The Big Apple Coaster
(Second floor)

Brooklyn Bridge

MGM GRAND STATION

NEW YORK–NEW YORK

Statue of Liberty

WEST TROPICANA AVENUE

EAST TROPICANA AVENUE

EXCALIBUR WAY

THE TROPICANA

Fun Dungeon
(Lower level)

EXCALIBUR

LUXOR DRIVE

STABLE ROAD

WEST RENO AVENUE

EAST RENO AVENUE

GILES ST

HAVEN ST

(THE STRIP)

MANDALAY BAY–EXCALIBUR MONORAIL

Titanic: The Artifact Exhibition
(Atrium level)

LUXOR

Bodies...The Exhibition
(Atrium level)

Sphinx

LUXOR DRIVE

Mandalay Place

LAS VEGAS BOULEVARD SOUTH

W. HACIENDA AVE

E. HACIENDA AVE

EAST HACIENDA AVENUE

SHOPS
Las Vegas Premium
  Outlets (South) ... 3
The Shoppes at
  Mandalay Place ... 1
Town Square ... 2

BARS & LOUNGES
Bar at Times Square ... 1
Foundation Room ... 7
Minus5 Ice Bar ... 5
Nine Fine Irishmen ... 2

CLUBS & MUSIC VENUES
Centra ... 4
Daylight Beach Club ... 8
Hakkasan ... 3
House of Blues ... 6

MANDALAY BAY

FOUR SEASONS

Moorea Beach Club

Shark Reef

SHOWS
Blue Man Group ... 5
  (on Atrium level)
Criss Angel –
  Mindfreak Live! ... 6
Jabbawockeez ... 3
Kà ... 1
Terry Fator ... 2
Tournament of Kings ... 4
  (on Lower level)

Little Church of the West

0 metres 250
0 yards 250

WEST RUSSELL ROAD

"Welcome to Fabulous Las Vegas" sign (0.5 mile), ② (1.5 miles) ▽ & ③ (2.5 miles)

Beyond that, however, there's little to distinguish the main casino floor. In the absence of noteworthy restaurants or shops, Luxor is best known for its clubs and bars, including *Flight*, a great place to drink cocktails and party.

Immediately upstairs, the so-called Atrium Level is home to two of Vegas's best permanent exhibitions – **Bodies** (see below) and **Titanic** – as well as a small food court. It's also the best vantage point from which to admire the pyramid's cavernous interior; only guests can access the higher levels.

Titanic: The Artifact Exhibition

MAP P.26, POCKET MAP A5
Atrium Level, Luxor, 3900 Las Vegas Blvd S Ⓦ luxor.mgmresorts.com/en/entertainment/titanic.html. Charge.

Held in an enclosed building upstairs in Luxor, **Titanic: The Artifact Exhibition** is the world's only permanent exhibition of items salvaged from the *Titanic*. Displays that also include mock-ups of the fabled Grand Staircase tell the full story of the great ship, from construction to destruction. Each visitor is invited to pose for a souvenir photo on the Staircase, and as you enter you receive a "boarding pass" named for a specific passenger. Only as you leave do you find out whether he or she survived the catastrophe.

Prize artefacts include the actual wheel at which the helmsman tried and failed to steer clear of the iceberg on April 14, 1912, and the Big Piece, a gigantic slab of side-hull that broke off C Deck as the ship sank, and which was raised from the ocean floor in 1998.

Bodies...The Exhibition

MAP P.26, POCKET MAP A5
Atrium Level, Luxor, 3900 Las Vegas Blvd S Ⓦ luxor.com/en/entertainment/bodies-the-exhibition.html. Charge.

You might expect **Bodies... The Exhibition** to be a gory horror show. In fact, despite the advertising images of goggle-eyed corpses, it provides a surprisingly serious museum-quality experience. You have to keep reminding yourself that what look like brightly coloured mannequins really are dead bodies that have been "plastinated" for permanent display. Some are posed as though in life, playing sports in perpetuity, others have been dissected to show particular features of their anatomy. Certain sections, like that in which an entire circulatory system, down to the tiniest capillary, has been teased out and dyed in different colours, have an astonishing beauty. The sight of fatally diseased organs displayed alongside healthy counterparts is much more sobering. Even if you've wandered in for a quick laugh, you may leave determined to change your life around – not that Las Vegas is necessarily the best place to start.

Excalibur

MAP P.26, POCKET MAP B4
3850 Las Vegas Blvd S Ⓦ excalibur.com.

Built in 1990, **Excalibur** remains the most visible reminder of

Bodies...The Exhibition

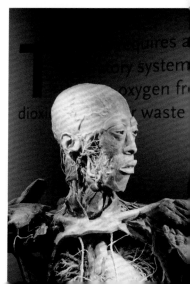

the era when Las Vegas briefly reinvented itself as a vast children's playground. With its jam-packed, multi-coloured turrets and ring of clunky battlements it doesn't so much look like a castle, as like a child's drawing of a castle – and to be more specific still, a drawing of Walt Disney's version of Sleeping Beauty's castle. In fact, the architect responsible, Veldon Simpson, who later went on to design both Luxor and the MGM Grand, had travelled around Europe visiting hundreds of real-life castles. He ultimately settled on the same model used by Disney, Neuschwanstein in Bavaria, a whimsical hybrid of French château and stern German fortress. Only a nit-picker would mention that the original Excalibur was a sword, not a castle.

These days, Excalibur is less child-oriented than it used to be. Its primary function for current owners MGM seems to be a kind of gateway to draw visitors towards the southern end of the Strip, complementing the free Mandalay Bay-Excalibur Express Tram to Luxor (see page 25) and Mandalay Bay (see page 24), prominent outside, with an easy indoor walkway to those properties further back. You access that by heading onto the upper level from the casino, lured ever onwards along the corridor by boutiques and fast-food places.

As Excalibur generally offers some of the Strip's least expensive hotel rooms, it caters largely to low-budget tour groups and families. That can result in a slightly jarring clash between its remaining child-friendly Arthurian theming, which includes the knights-a-jousting *Tournament of Kings* (see page 37), and blue-collar adult entertainment such as *Dick's Last Resort* bar and the *Thunder From Down Under* male stripper revue (performers from the latter often hang around the entrance for photo ops). Its lowest level, below the casino floor, is occupied by the **Fun Dungeon**, a jumble of fairground stalls, carnival amusements and arcade games.

Much of the upstairs, officially known as the Castle Walk Level, is taken up by a huge **food court**, which includes a massive *Krispy Kreme* doughnut bakery – where all the kitchen action is open to passers-by – and a *Cinnabon* outlet. It's also home to the *Excalibur Buffet* and assorted souvenir "shoppes".

The Tropicana

MAP P.26, POCKET MAP C4
3801 Las Vegas Blvd S Ⓦ troplv.com.
Built in 1957 and standing proudly aloof a mile south of the Strip, the **Tropicana** swiftly became a byword for luxury. It was also renowned from the start as being in the pocket of the Mob and spent twenty years under investigation for the "skimming" of casino profits, money laundering and other Mafia-related skulduggery.

Although it's now poised at the country's busiest crossroads, the

"Welcome to Fabulous Las Vegas"

Familiar no doubt from every Las Vegas movie or TV show you've ever seen, the "Welcome to Fabulous Las Vegas" sign is an obligatory photo op for every visitor, just over half a mile south of Mandalay Bay. To minimize the risk of accidents, only cars heading south, away from the city, can access the narrow patch in between the north- and southbound carriageways of the Strip. It's unwise to try walking this far in summer. Expect to queue to get your turn with the sign.

The New York–New York Hotel and Casino

Tropicana has long struggled to compete with its mighty MGM-owned neighbours – Excalibur (see page 27), the MGM Grand (see page 30), and New York–New York (see right). Barely rescued from bankruptcy in 2008, it was given a $125-million makeover intended to restore its tropical-playground image and add something of the feel of Miami's South Beach. Among the casualties of that process was its fabled topless revue, the Folies Bergère, which ended its residency shortly before its fiftieth anniversary.

While it's looking much crisper and brighter than before, the Tropicana still can't match the latest Strip giants. Unrealised hopes that it would blossom as a nightlife destination were further dented by Covid. Instead, it remains slightly apart, with its strongest feature being an extensive pool complex that's open to guests only. Bally's has since taken over at the Tropicana and in 2023, the latest in a string of revival plans proposed building a new baseball stadium over much of the existing site. While this is far from a done deal,

it's further proof that Vegas has little room for sentiment.

New York–New York

MAP P.26, POCKET MAP B3
3790 Las Vegas Blvd S
Ⓦ newyorknewyork.com.

The first, and arguably the best, of Las Vegas's modern breed of replica "cities", **New York–New York** opened in 1997. Its exterior consists of a squeezed-up, half-sized rendition of the Manhattan skyline as it looked in the 1950s. The interior, which makes no attempt to correspond to the specific "buildings" outside, holds a smaller than average casino, plus a dining and nightlife district intended to evoke Greenwich Village.

Despite the broad Brooklyn Bridge that stretches along the Strip sidewalk, and the Empire State and Chrysler buildings etched against the Nevada sky, the most iconic feature of the facade is the **Statue of Liberty**, facing the intersection with Tropicana Avenue. Unlike the other elements here it's actually twice the height of the real-life statue.

This spot never hosted a replica of the World Trade Center, but ad hoc memorials appeared here after September 11, 2001.

Although New York–New York has lost some of its original playful theming – sightseers once stepped off the Strip to find themselves in Central Park at night, with owls peeping down from the trees – touches of Big Apple whimsy were restored to the rooms during an extensive renovation in 2023. Elsewhere, things are enlivened with stylish Art Deco motifs.

New York–New York isn't served by any monorail, but pedestrians pass through one corner en-route between the pedestrian bridges to Excalibur and the MGM Grand. Perhaps to tempt them to stay, the areas nearest the Strip host an abundance of bars, pubs and food outlets. Much of the second floor is taken up by the Arcade, a rather ramshackle assortment of sideshows, games and kids' attractions.

The Big Apple Coaster

MAP P.26, POCKET MAP B3

New York–New York, 3790 Las Vegas Blvd S Ⓦ newyorknewyork.com. Charge.
From the moment you catch a glimpse of New York–New York, you'll almost certainly also see – and hear – the tiny little yellow cabs that loop and race around its skyscraper towers. Previously known first as the Manhattan Express, then simply as The Roller Coaster, and now re-renamed **The Big Apple Coaster**, it operates from a replica subway station on the casino's upper floor. Speeding at 67mph, plunging over 200ft and rolling like a jet fighter, it's a serious thrill ride no theme-park fan should miss.

MGM Grand

MAP P.26, POCKET MAP C3
3799 Las Vegas Blvd S Ⓦ mgmgrand.com.
The enormous **MGM Grand** casino has been through many changes since it opened in 1993. Back then, it attracted huge publicity as the largest hotel in the world and the first to incorporate its own theme park. It was also the location of the legendary 1997 boxing fight during which Mike Tyson bit Evander Holyfield's ear.

The MGM Grand casino

MGM Grand's casino

These days, however, the MGM Grand keeps a lower profile, and it would be hard to say quite what identity it's aiming for anymore. All traces of the theme park have long since vanished, while only the general preponderance of green now recalls the property's initial *Wizard of Oz* theme. With its original 5005 rooms boosted by the addition of the three all-suite *Signature* towers, it's surpassed in size only by the Venetian-Palazzo combination. Only in Las Vegas could such a behemoth seem to blend into the background.

One reason for this may be that with so many guests on site, the MGM Grand simply doesn't need to lure visitors in. It still boasts a fabulous array of dining and entertainment options, which includes the stunning Cirque de Soleil show *Kà*, and the three Michelin-starred *Joël Robuchon Restaurant*, where the $485 Degustation Menu is said to be among the world's most expensive prix fixes.

MGM Resorts occasionally overhaul the Grand, cutting shows and events that aren't making the grade, such as their CSI TV-show-inspired experience. Removing the live lions displayed in a glass enclosure was, however, a humane step towards protecting the species that has famously lent its image to MGM for so long.

The Hunger Games: The Exhibition

MAP P.26, POCKET MAP E2
MGM Grand, 3799 Las Vegas Blvd S
Ⓦ thehungergamesexhibition.com. Charge.
Set well back from the MGM Grand's Strip entrance, **The Hunger Games: The Exhibition** is an interactive family attraction aimed at fans of the books and movies. It allows you to step into the world of Panem, with recreations of key locations such as District 13 and President Snow's office.

An exhibition of memorabilia from the films includes many of the original costumes worn by the cast and your ticket allows you to step (figuratively) into the shoes of Katniss Everdeen at the hands-on digital archery training facility.

Shops

Las Vegas Premium Outlets (South)

MAP P.26, POCKET MAP B13
7400 Las Vegas Blvd S
Ⓦ premiumoutlets.com.

The sort of mall you might find beside the highway on the outskirts of any town in America, Las Vegas Premium Outlets (South), three miles south of Mandalay Bay, offers no-frills, no-nonsense shopping at Banana Republic, Gap, Nike and the like. For visitors with the use of a car, it's not a bad option for picking up everyday items at factory outlet prices to take back home. There's a basic fast-food court, grill and Italian-style pizzeria.

The Shoppes at Mandalay Place

MAP P.26, POCKET MAP B6
Mandalay Bay, 3950 Las Vegas Blvd S
Ⓦ mandalaybay.com.

Arranged along the indoor hallway that connects Mandalay Bay with Luxor – a fair walk from the centre of either, and from the express tram too – The Shoppes at Mandalay Place does not rank among Las Vegas's premier shopping malls. Instead, it's a rather haphazard mix of big names such as Guinness Store, Lush Cosmetics and Swarovski, and smart boutiques, galleries and novelty stores, plus several bars and restaurants.

Town Square

MAP P.26, POCKET MAP B13
6605 Las Vegas Blvd S
Ⓦ mytownsquarelasvegas.com.

Especially popular with locals who prefer to steer clear of the Strip, Town Square, three miles south of Mandalay Bay, is a rarity in Las Vegas, designed to be experienced as an outdoor "neighbourhood" rather than an air-conditioned enclave. Visitors from further afield may be less enthused by its attempt to evoke the feel of a "European village". Big stores include H&M, a Whole Foods supermarket, Sephora and an Apple Store; there are also some unremarkable restaurants and a cinema.

Buffet

The Buffet at Luxor

MAP P.26, POCKET MAP B6
3900 Las Vegas Blvd S Ⓦ luxor.com.

After the pandemic, some of Vegas' once-legendary buffets didn't return. Others returned with reduced hours covering breakfast, brunch and lunch, such as The Buffet at Luxor. Located in the casino's lower level, there are pizza, carved meat and omelette stations, a salad bar, and a dessert cart. An additional all-you-can-drink bloody Mary and mimosa option is also available. $

Restaurants

America

MAP P.26, POCKET MAP B3
New York–New York, 3790 Las Vegas Blvd S
Ⓦ newyorknewyork.com.

While serious foodies will find nothing remarkable about this 24-hour diner, it's a great place to bring kids, or Las Vegas first-timers, thanks to the colossal, cartoon-like relief map of the USA that hangs from the ceiling. Serving signature dishes from all over the country, including Atlantic salmon salad and Southwest mac n' cheese, there's food to match many an appetite. $$

Border Grill

MAP P.26, POCKET MAP B8
Mandalay Bay, 3950 Las Vegas Blvd S
Ⓦ bordergrill.com.

Serving light and zestful "modern Mexican" cuisine that's a perfect match for its sun-kissed indoor-outdoor setting, this poolside veteran serves lunchtime salads,

Barbecue Shrimp at Emeril's New Orleans Fish House

tacos and *tortas* (flatbreads), and larger dinner plates like Yucatan pork or vegan portobello mushroom mulitas. Border brunch on weekends includes unlimited small plates with an option to add bottomless mimosas and micheladas. $$

Emeril's New Orleans Fish House

MAP P.26, POCKET MAP E2
MGM Grand, 3799 Las Vegas Blvd S
Ⓦ emerils.com.

Rich New Orleans flavours in a modern setting, courtesy of TV chef Emeril Lagasse. As the name suggests, the emphasis is on seafood, with Creole shrimp among appetizers and Carolina gold jambalaya on the mains menu, but you can also get fried chicken or a prime rib-eye steak. If you don't have a dinner reservation, they should be able to seat you after 8.30pm. $$$

Fleur

MAP P.26, POCKET MAP B7
Mandalay Bay, 3950 Las Vegas Blvd S
Ⓦ mandalaybay.com.

Once notorious for selling a $5000 foie gras burger, Hubert Keller's modern tapas restaurant today is branded more as the kind of place to have a quiet meal away from the brash Vegas atmosphere. A sumptuous menu features Comte gnocchi or scallops with bacon jam. Steaks have pride of place on the menu and can be enhanced with scallops or lobster tail. $$$

Hussong's Cantina

MAP P.26, POCKET MAP B6
Mandalay Bay, 3930 Las Vegas Blvd S
Ⓦ hussongslasvegas.com.

An outpost of the Mexican original that's said (apocryphally) to have invented the margarita, *Hussong's* is as much a bar as a restaurant. Yet the Tex-Mex-style food itself is surprisingly good, with flautas, fajitas, chimichangas, and nachos. Don't miss the grilled corn, which is dusted with cheese flakes. $

Il Fornaio

MAP P.26, POCKET MAP B3
New York–New York, 3790 Las Vegas Blvd S
Ⓦ ilfornaio.com/lasvegas.

While *Il Fornaio* is open for decent Italian food from lunch through the evening, in-the-know locals love it best of all in the morning, when you can enjoy a wonderful sit-down breakfast or simply pop into the separate deli/bakery next door for fresh bread and espresso coffee. Be sure to check out the happy hour specials. $$$

Lupo by Wolfgang Puck

MAP P.26, POCKET MAP B7
Mandalay Bay, 3950 Las Vegas Blvd S
Ⓦ wolfgangpuck.com.

Austrian-American celebrity chef Wolfgang Puck's Rome-inspired cuisine is served up with flair in an airy space with an open kitchen. The menu is split into pizzas, pasta dishes such as ravioli al formaggio with sheep's milk ricotta and San Marzano tomato sauce, and *secondi*, including pan seared Alaskan halibut or braised veal osso buco. $$$

Morimoto Las Vegas

MAP P.26, POCKET MAP D3
MGM Grand, 3799 Las Vegas Blvd S
Ⓦ mgmgrand.com.

This suave establishment from Japanese Iron Chef Masaharu Morimoto focusses on the dining experience as much as the delicate ingredients. Plates of sushi and sashimi, dollops of caviar and cuts of glistening sashimi are part of the a la carte experience, while the teppanyaki grill area draws diners seeking an interactive experience as your chef prepares dishes right in front of you. $$$$

Oakville Tuscan Grill

MAP P.26, POCKET MAP C4
Tropicana, 3801 Las Vegas Blvd S
Ⓦ troplv.com.

A place for seafood and steaks is not going to stand out as novel or original in Las Vegas, but Oakville Tuscan Grill is known to do both exceptionally well. Start with a creamy burrata, before exploring the steaks and their enhancements, including asparagus and crab. House seafood specialties include gulf snapper on a bed of quinoa, pancetta and cauliflower. $$$

Tap Sports Bar

MAP P.26, POCKET MAP D3
MGM Grand, 3799 Las Vegas Blvd S
Ⓦ mgmgrand.com.

If you want to tap into some of the local sporting action, the Vegas Golden Knights ice hockey team games are screened at Tap Sports Bar to eager fans. Draft beers and sport-themed cocktails such as The Owner (made with bourbon, bitters and Luxardo cherry) accompany comfort food in the form of burgers (beef, bacon and Beyond options), cheesesteaks and tacos (carne asada, beer battered fish or chicken). $$

Tom Colicchio's Craftsteak

MAP P.26, POCKET MAP E2
MGM Grand, 3799 Las Vegas Blvd S
Ⓦ craftsteaklasvegas.com.

Serious carnivores swear this dinner-only steakhouse serves the best beef in Las Vegas, in melt-in-your-mouth inch-thick cuts. Order a la carte; there's lobster salad as an appetizer and steaks of many kinds. Set menus range from domestic Angus beef to Japanese Wagyu surf & turf. $$$$

Bars and lounges

Bar at Times Square

MAP P.26, POCKET MAP B3
New York–New York, 3790 Las Vegas Blvd S
Ⓦ newyorknewyork.com.

If you like your nights out sophisticated or edgy, steer clear of this raucous sing-along bar alongside New York–New York's main casino floor; if you prefer to scream along at the top of your voice as two pianists go head-to-head, playing whatever requests spring to their tipsy audience's mind, you're in the right place.

Minus5 Ice Bar

Foundation Room

MAP P.26, POCKET MAP B7
Mandalay Bay, 3950 Las Vegas Blvd S
Ⓦ mandalaybay.com.
Sophistication can be found on
the top floor of the Mandalay
at the Foundation Room. With
lounge tables looking out over the
city, you can sip cocktails from
this bar's vast mixology menu,
including house specials such as
the ginza fashioned, alongside all
of the classic cocktails.

Minus5 Ice Bar

MAP P.26, POCKET MAP B6
Mandalay Bay, 3930 Las Vegas Blvd S
Ⓦ minus5experience.com.
This funny, gimmicky bar is exactly
what it says it is – everything is
made of ice, from walls to glasses
(though the couches are spread
with deer skins). Customers
are loaned jackets, gloves and
boots to tolerate the minus 5°C
temperature.

Nine Fine Irishmen

MAP P.26, POCKET MAP C3
New York–New York, 3790 Las Vegas Blvd S
Ⓦ ninefineirishmen.com.

This genuine Irish pub was shipped
in pieces from Ireland, then rebuilt
in Vegas to celebrate Irish beer,
food and live Celtic music every
night of the week. A small patio out
on the Strip looks over "Brooklyn
Bridge". Traditional Irish fare from
the kitchen includes shepherd's pie,
and lamb and Guinness stew served
with vegetables.

Clubs and music venues

Centra

MAP P.26, POCKET MAP B6
Luxor, 3900 Las Vegas Blvd S Ⓦ luxor.com.
Located within the Luxor resort,
this round-the-clock bar is a great
place to enjoy some casual drinks
while you play poker or video slot
games. Must-see sporting events
are broadcast live from the venue's
screens.

Daylight Beach Club

MAP P.26, POCKET MAP B8
Mandalay Bay, 3950 Las Vegas Blvd S
Ⓦ mandalaybay.com.

Mandalay Bay has one of the biggest pool areas on the Strip and the result are a handful of exclusive beach clubs where you can purchase access to poolside cabanas and deck chairs. Every weekend, DJs get Daylight's pool parties going, alongside live hip hop and reggaeton performances. The perfect way to pass an afternoon before hitting one of the other clubs later in the evening.

Hakkasan

MAP P.26, POCKET MAP D3
MGM Grand, 3799 Las Vegas Blvd S
Ⓦ hakkasan.com.
Said to be the largest club in the world, an offshoot of what was originally a Chinese restaurant in London, this colossal, multi-level place incorporates two separate full-sized nightclubs, plus all sorts of dining rooms, ultra-lounges and private gardens; superstar DJs attract up to 7500 clubbers at weekends.

House of Blues

MAP P.26, POCKET MAP B6
Mandalay Bay, 3950 Las Vegas Blvd S
Ⓦ houseofblues.com.
The national *House of Blues* music chain's Las Vegas outlet is located in the heart of Mandalay Bay. This live music venue has a funky, Louisiana voodoo-esque vibe to it, with a capacity of 1300 making for some lively shows. Individual touring artists hold concerts, interspersed with longer residencies. Carlos Santana splits the difference with two-week runs every few months.

Shows

Blue Man Group

MAP P.26, POCKET MAP B6
Luxor, 3900 Las Vegas Blvd S
Ⓦ blueman.com. Charge.
The hilariously postmodern Blue Men are Las Vegas favourites;

kids love their craziness, adults their cleverness. Mute and lurid blue from head to toe, they combine paint-splashing, cereal-spewing clowning with pounding percussion and amazing visual effects.

Criss Angel – Mindfreak Live!

MAP P.26, POCKET MAP A6
Luxor, 3900 Las Vegas Blvd S Ⓦ luxor.com.
Charge.
Although *Mindfreak Live!* bears the Cirque brand, it's basically a showcase for everything Angel does best, blending close-up trickery with mind-blowing illusions to create a thrilling magic show. Beyond the pyrotechnics and heavy metal, he's essentially a hard-working, old-fashioned audience-pleaser.

Jabbawockeez

MAP P.26, POCKET MAP B3
MGM Grand, 3799 Las Vegas Blvd S
Ⓦ jbwkz.com. Charge.
Originating in San Diego as a hip-hop dance crew, this troupe of masked dancers transforms the MGM Grand's stage into a family-friendly carnival of collaborative movement. Expect innovative athletic moves, synchronized choreography, and punchy hip-hop beats.

Kà

MAP P.26, POCKET MAP D2
MGM Grand, 3799 Las Vegas Blvd S
Ⓦ cirquedusoleil.com. Charge.
There's more martial-arts muscularity to this Cirque spectacular than to their other, more ethereal offerings; sceptics are guaranteed to find the set-piece stunts enacted on its tilting, rotating stage absolutely jaw-dropping. Add in extraordinary puppetry and sumptuous costumes, and while the twins-in-jeopardy storyline may leave you unmoved, *Kà* is certain to expand your horizons.

Jabbawoockeez

Terry Fator

MAP P.64, POCKET MAP B3
New York–New York, 3790 Las Vegas Blvd S
Ⓦ newyorknewyork.com. Charge.
Yes, this middle-American
ventriloquist swaps corny jokes
with soft-toy puppets, but he
also has an extraordinary talent:
an astonishing five-octave
singing voice that delivers perfect
impressions of artists from Ozzy
Osbourne to Etta James – all
without moving his lips. Despite
rocketing to fame and fortune
since he won *America's Got Talent*
in 2007, he is still likeable and
down-to-earth.

Tournament of Kings

MAP P.26, POCKET MAP A4
Excalibur, 3850 Las Vegas Blvd S
Ⓦ excalibur.com. Charge.
This swashbuckling swords-and-
slapstick supper show plunges
family audiences into a jousting
contest, complete with villainous
black knights and maidens in peril.
Ideal for anyone who'd rather eat
chicken with their fingers than sit
through Shakespeare.

Wedding chapel

Little Church of the West

MAP P.26, POCKET MAP C9
4617 Las Vegas Blvd S
Ⓦ littlechurchofthewest.com.
This cute little chapel really is
old, by Las Vegas standards; built
for the Last Frontier casino in
1942, it has since migrated south
to a spot half a mile beyond
Mandalay Bay. With its tranquil
garden, it feels a world away from
the big-casino chapels. Basic
packages include the "Ace of
Hearts" while premium includes
the "Desert Stardust" with all the
nuptial frills.

CityCenter and around

When MGM Resorts opened the CityCenter complex, in 2009, the aim was to add a whole new neighbourhood to Las Vegas, giving the city a new kind of sleek, corporate architecture. By building a self-contained enclave set back from the Strip, they would vastly increase the value of what was previously unused land, and finally make it possible to expand east–west. A massive financial gamble, the project involved a huge new casino, Aria; a high-end shopping mall, Crystals; and several hotel-and-condo skyscrapers. A new neighbourhood has indeed appeared, stretching from the open-air Park in the south, adjoining the Park MGM (with NoMad Hotel occupying the top floors), as far as the now-veteran Bellagio to the north. The one fly in MGM's ointment is the brash new Cosmopolitan, cheekily added to the one tiny speck of Strip real estate that MGM didn't own.

Park MGM

MAP P.40, POCKET MAP C2
3770 Las Vegas Blvd S ⓦ parkmgm.com.
With the unveiling of CityCenter, the low-profile **Monte Carlo** casino became increasingly prominent in the plans of owners MGM.

The space between the former Monte Carlo and New York–New York has been transformed into a largely pedestrianized plaza known as **The Park**, and is home to the huge, multi-purpose **T-Mobile Arena** (see page 47). In 2018,

The Park

the Monte Carlo was re-branded as the **Park MGM**. Alongside the **Dolby Live (formerly Park Theater)** concert venue (see page 47), the new complex houses an Italian marketplace, **Eataly**, with restaurants and food counters, and an almost 300-room boutique hotel, **NoMad**.

Crystals

MAP P.40, POCKET MAP B1 & F9
3720 Las Vegas Blvd S
ⓦ theshopsatcrystals.com.

As the one public component of CityCenter to abut the Strip, **Crystals** certainly catches the eye. Designed by Daniel Libeskind, its jagged, colourful facade makes a contrast to the white walls and air-conditioned cool of its interior. Its primary role is as a (hugely expensive) shopping mall, **The Shops at Crystals** (see page 44).

Purely as a spectacle, however, Crystals is well worth a quick walk-through. At one point, it was planned as an urban park, and it features some extravagant, playful wooden structures, including the intricate 70ft **Treehouse**, home to the stylish *Mastro's Ocean Club* restaurant (see page 45), as well as a pair of arching wooden "pods".

There's also plenty of water on show, including the swirling glass-encased **fountains** on the lower floor, and some dazzling **sculptures** of neon light.

The Cosmopolitan

MAP P.40, POCKET MAP F9
3708 Las Vegas Blvd S
ⓦ cosmopolitanlasvegas.com.

At first glance, most Las Vegas visitors assume that **The Cosmopolitan**, facing Planet Hollywood (see page 48) across the Strip, is just one more piece of the modernist jigsaw puzzle that comprises CityCenter. It's not; it's an entirely separate luxury casino-hotel, stacked up vertically rather than sprawling horizontally, and impishly squeezed atop the car

Crystals

park of the former Jockey Club (which MGM never managed to buy up), slap in front of CityCenter.

Since opening in 2010, the Cosmopolitan has made itself very much at home in this prime spot, seducing visitors with its glitzy architectural flourishes, high-profile **Marquee** nightclub (see page 47), excellent array of appealing restaurants just steps away from the Strip, and general evocation of glamorous days gone by. In the evenings especially, its buzzing public spaces tend to jostle with excited crowds.

The Cosmopolitan is a throwback to the old Las Vegas, when each casino was separately owned and run, acted like the rest of the city didn't exist, saw its business as being all about gambling and nightlife rather than shopping, and aimed to keep visitors on site by making it all but impossible to find the exits. Be warned that the Cosmopolitan also has the last laugh on CityCenter: while you might understandably assume that you could simply walk all the way

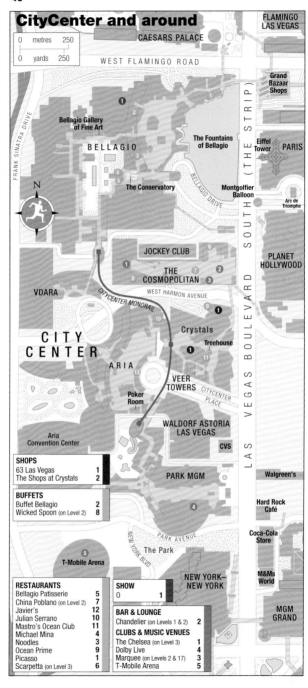

CityCenter and around

| 0 | metres | 250 |
| 0 | yards | 250 |

FLAMINGO LAS VEGAS

CAESARS PALACE

WEST FLAMINGO ROAD

Grand Bazaar Shops

Bellagio Gallery of Fine Art

BELLAGIO

The Fountains of Bellagio

Eiffel Tower   PARIS

The Conservatory

Montgolfier Balloon

Arc de Triomphe

FRANK SINATRA DRIVE

(THE STRIP)

LAS VEGAS BOULEVARD SOUTH

PLANET HOLLYWOOD

JOCKEY CLUB

THE COSMOPOLITAN

BELLAGIO DRIVE

VDARA

CITYCENTER MONORAIL

WEST HARMON AVENUE

CITY CENTER

ARIA

Crystals

Treehouse

Poker Room

VEER TOWERS

CITYCENTER PLACE

WALDORF ASTORIA LAS VEGAS

CVS

Aria Convention Center

PARK MGM

Walgreen's

Hard Rock Café

Coca-Cola Store

PARK AVENUE

NEW YORK BLVD

The Park

T-Mobile Arena

NEW YORK– NEW YORK

M&Ms World

MGM GRAND

SHOPS	
63 Las Vegas	1
The Shops at Crystals	2

BUFFETS	
Buffet Bellagio	2
Wicked Spoon (on Level 2)	8

RESTAURANTS	
Bellagio Patisserie	5
China Poblano (on Level 2)	7
Javier's	12
Julian Serrano	10
Mastro's Ocean Club	11
Michael Mina	4
Noodles	3
Ocean Prime	9
Picasso	1
Scarpetta (on Level 3)	6

SHOW	
O	1

BAR & LOUNGE	
Chandelier (on Levels 1 & 2)	2
CLUBS & MUSIC VENUES	
The Chelsea (on Level 3)	1
Dolby Live	4
Marquee (on Levels 2 & 17)	3
T-Mobile Arena	5

through the building and reach Aria (see page 41), you can't – there's no pedestrian through route.

Aria

MAP P.40, POCKET MAP B1
3730 Las Vegas Blvd S ⓦ aria.com.

Although the CityCenter "neighbourhood" is supposed to be easy to explore on foot, you're only likely to visit **Aria**, the casino at its heart, if you make a very deliberate effort to reach it. Pedestrians can get here outdoors by following its hot, exposed approach road 250 yards west from the Strip, or more comfortably indoors, via the Crystals mall or the much longer walkways through Bellagio (see page 42) and the Park MGM (see page 38). A gleaming sci-fi **monorail** also connects Aria with both those properties, but the stations are so far back from the Strip that you gain very little by using it unless you're staying in one of these resorts.

From the outside, with its sleek, curving skyscrapers, Aria looks more like a sophisticated big-city corporate HQ than a casino. The traffic circle in front of its main entrance features a pulsating **fountain**, while to the left, more water cascades down a sleek, glistening black wall, 24ft tall.

Aria also identifies itself more with, say, Chicago than Las Vegas, by eschewing billboards, video screens and neon in favour of prestigious **contemporary art**. Sculptors represented include Henry Moore, one of whose signature abstractions stands in the tiny gap between Aria and Crystals; Claes Oldenburg, responsible for the giant typewriter eraser near the Strip; Antony Gormley, whose *Feeling Material* hangs from the ceiling; and Maya Lin, whose 84ft silver casting of the Colorado River stretches above the check-in desks.

While Aria's dazzling modernism is certainly a welcome contrast with traditional Las Vegas aesthetics, in the end, of course, it's all in the service of Mammon – and more specifically, gambling. There's

Aria casino

Musical fountains at Bellagio

plenty more cutting-edge design to admire as you walk through the casino proper – don't miss the **Poker Room**, fringed by gigantic golden playing cards – but there's little reason to linger unless your intention is to gamble.

Both the upper and lower levels of Aria hold a fine roster of restaurants, bars and cafés, but there are very few shops. Devoid of slots and gaming tables, the upper level can feel cavernously empty unless the **Convention Center** is in full swing.

When Aria opened it was home to a Cirque du Soleil tribute show to Elvis Presley. An unlikely fit for such a forward-looking property, the show swiftly ended its run, as did its replacement, Cirque's **Zarkana**. With the showroom now closed, Aria has shifted its focus to the Dolby Live venue instead.

Bellagio

MAP P.40, POCKET MAP F7
3600 Las Vegas Blvd S Ⓦ bellagio.com.
Ranking high among Las Vegas's absolute must-see casinos, **Bellagio** proudly surveys the Strip across the graceful dancing fountains of its own broad, semicircular lake. This cream-coloured vision of Italian elegance was unveiled in 1998 as the final great flourish of the twentieth century's fastest-growing new city. It was the handiwork of legendary entrepreneur Steve Wynn, who spared no expense in his bid to follow his success with the Mirage (see page 62) by building the greatest hotel the world had ever seen. His original idea was to model it on a French Mediterranean beach and call it Beau Rivage; that changed after he visited the village of Bellagio, beside Lake Como in Italy.

Although Wynn himself is no longer at the helm – when MGM bought out his Mirage corporation in 2000, he took the money and ran down the street to start again – Bellagio is still going strong, racking up the highest turnover and biggest profits in the city. It's also larger than ever, having thrust a tentacle southwards to create an indoor walkway down to CityCenter. As Bellagio's northeast corner is just a few steps across a pedestrian bridge from Caesars Palace (see page 51), many sightseers use it as a corridor to stay out of the sun as they head south, creating a constant flow of visitors.

Almost all of Bellagio's Strip facade is taken up with waterfront restaurants, so once you're inside you won't see much of the lake. Similarly, its colonnaded pool area is only open to guests. Even so, the sheer opulence of the main casino floor is astounding, and several of the public areas should not be missed. In addition to the **Conservatory**, be sure to walk through the hotel lobby, where a vast chandelier of multicoloured glass flowers, created by sculptor Dale Chihuly, swarms across the ceiling. And take a glance behind the check-in counter to see the Roman gardens, accessible to employees only.

When Bellagio first opened, the management briefly attempted to impose a dress code and bar the children of non-guests. Las Vegas's democratic open-to-all traditions soon put paid to that policy, however, so there's nothing snooty about the crowds you'll see window shopping in the exclusive stores of the small Via Bellagio shopping arcade, or gasping at the menu prices for its magnificent but undeniably expensive restaurants. Other than the building itself, the two most popular attractions that bring in visitors from elsewhere are the **buffet** (see page 44) and Cirque du Soleil's long-running, breathtaking water spectacular, **O** (see page 47).

The Fountains of Bellagio

MAP P.40, POCKET MAP F7
Bellagio, 3600 Las Vegas Blvd S. Free.
Even when it's lying dormant, Bellagio's ice-blue eight-acre lake is an impressive spectacle in the Nevada desert. When it erupts into a balletic extravaganza of jetting **fountains**, as it does from early afternoon until midnight daily, it's the best free show in town. The sky-high spurts and streams are accompanied by booming music – mostly songs from Broadway shows and popular classics. For anyone other than diners in the expensive waterfront restaurants, the best views are from the Strip sidewalk (stake your place early), the top of the Eiffel Tower in Paris (see page 49) or from the guest rooms in either Paris (see page 48) or the Cosmopolitan (see page 39).

The Conservatory

MAP P.40, POCKET MAP E8
Bellagio, 3600 Las Vegas Blvd S. Free.
Ever since Bellagio opened, its magnificent **Conservatory** has been considered one of the major sights of the city. A glassed-over courtyard ringed by galleries and restaurants, it's repeatedly transformed by a huge team of gardeners into extravagant, themed shows that include bizarre whimsical props amid an extraordinary array of living plants. The five separate seasonal displays start with the Chinese New Year and then celebrate spring, summer, autumn and winter. During the week it takes to dismantle each show and prepare the next, there's nothing to see.

Bellagio Gallery of Fine Art

MAP P.40, POCKET MAP E7
Bellagio, 3600 Las Vegas Blvd S
ⓦ bellagio.com. Charge.
Originally home to Steve Wynn's own art collection, the **Bellagio Gallery of Fine Art** managed to survive Wynn's departure and continues to put on changing exhibitions that generally last for around six months. The entrance fee is high for such a small space, although rotating exhibits generally include works by high profile artists, including Andy Warhol, Claude Monet, Regina Bogat, Salvador Dalí, and Ai Weiwei.

Shops

63 Las Vegas

MAP P.40, POCKET MAP F9
4th Floor, 63 Las Vegas, 3716 Las Vegas
Blvd S ⓦ 63lasvegas.com.

Designed to complement, rather
than compete with Crystals, Aria's
63 Las Vegas is a CityCenter
shopping experience aimed at the
everyday visitor. Fully open to the
public in 2024, it includes retail
and restaurants across four floors.
At the time of writing, the Museum
of Illusions was also due to open
here.

The Shops at Crystals

MAP P.40, POCKET MAP F9
3720 Las Vegas Blvd S ⓦ simon.com/mall/
theshops-at-crystals.

Pitched at Las Vegas's proverbial
"whales"– high-rolling big
spenders – the glitzy Shops at
Crystals makes no bones about
being very high-end indeed.
With its sparkling white walls,
and exquisite sculptural features,
few dare stray into boutiques
belonging to designers such as
Karl Lagerfeld.

Buffets

Buffet Bellagio

MAP P.40, POCKET MAP E7
Bellagio, 3600 Las Vegas Blvd S
ⓦ bellagio.com.

The first "gourmet buffet" in
town sparked standards, and less
happily prices, to rise all over
Las Vegas. While no longer quite
as exceptional, it still features
an amazing array of food. For
breakfast you can have salmon
smoked or baked, and omelettes
cooked to order, with fillings such
as crabmeat. $$

Wicked Spoon

MAP P.40, POCKET MAP J6
Level 2, The Cosmopolitan, 3708 Las Vegas
Blvd S ⓦ cosmopolitanlasvegas.com.

Although the Cosmopolitan's buffet
is hard to find, right at the back
upstairs, plenty of visitors make
their way here to enjoy a wide
range of carefully prepared cuisines.
Most are served as individual
portions, though you can take as
many as you like. There's no dinner,
but it's open for breakfast and
lunch on weekdays and brunch at
the weekend. $$

Restaurants

Bellagio Patisserie

MAP P.40, POCKET MAP E8
Bellagio, 3600 Las Vegas Blvd S
ⓦ bellagio.com. No reservations.

It takes real self-discipline to
walk past the delectable Bellagio
Patisserie. Start your day with a
breakfast of pastries, omelettes
and freshly brewed coffee. For
lunch tuck into sandwiches, with
crepes for dessert, and sweeten
your journey home with a box of
macarons or tasty chocolates. $

China Poblano

MAP P.40, POCKET MAP K6
Level 2, The Cosmopolitan, 3708 Las Vegas
Blvd S ⓦ chinapoblano.com.

The concept of combining Asia
and Mexico goes back a long way
– *china poblana* was a traditional
urban dress style worn by women
in Mexico. Here, in what looks
like a street café, it is Chinese and
Mexican cuisines that are blended.
There are options for vegetarians,
such as the Twenty Vegetable
Fried Rice dish (fried rice, egg,
pea shoots and twenty seasonal
vegetables); see if you can count
them all. $$

Javier's

MAP P.40, POCKET MAP B1
Casino Level, Aria, 3730 Las Vegas Blvd S
ⓦ aria.com.

Spectacular Mexican restaurant,
complete with terrifying wooden
carvings, serving all the standard
dishes, scrupulously prepared. Try

Bellagio Patisserie

the build-your-own-tacos plate for two, or opt for one of the more inventive variations such as lobster enchiladas, or the shrimp, steak and seafood mains. $$

Julian Serrano

MAP P.40, POCKET MAP F9
Casino Level, Aria, 3730 Las Vegas Blvd S
ⓦ aria.com.
One of Las Vegas's biggest hits of recent years, this beautiful tapas bar tastes even better than it looks, with its warm décor and quirky, modern entranceway. Tapas are divided into vegetables, meat, chicken and eggs, and seafood categories. Highlights include fabulous creations like the cocoa butter balls filled with chilled gazpacho. Larger mains include paella for two. $$$

Mastro's Ocean Club

MAP P.40, POCKET MAP B1
Crystals, 3720 Las Vegas Blvd S
ⓦ mastrosrestaurants.com.
Even the new Las Vegas still has a penchant for a good old-fashioned steakhouse, though this one stands out not so much for its heavy-duty rib-eyes as its amazing setting. Reserve early and you get to dine in the bowers of Crystals' whimsical wooden Treehouse. $$$

Michael Mina

MAP P.40, POCKET MAP E8
Bellagio 3600 Las Vegas Blvd S
ⓦ michaelmina.net.
In his flagship, Michelin-starred restaurant, adjoining Bellagio's Conservatory, Egyptian-born Michael Mina continues to reinvent his tried and tested classics. Expect starters such as tuna tartare with mint and Scotch bonnet, while mains range from filo-crusted sole to Mina's signature lobster pot pie. The chef also presents two tasting menus, as well as a vegetarian version (among

Scarpetta

Vegas' best meat-free fine dining experiences), with optional wine pairings. $$$$

Noodles

MAP P.40, POCKET MAP F8
Bellagio, 3600 Las Vegas Blvd S
Ⓦ bellagio.com.

Bellagio's casual, walk-ins only, pan-Asian diner, off the main casino floor behind the *Baccarat* bar, is well worth seeking out. Its intriguing decor sets a cosy tone and the food, which covers Thai, Vietnamese, Chinese and Japanese, is no disappointment. Noodle and rice dishes fill the main menu, while dim sum are available during lunch at weekends. $$

Ocean Prime

MAP P.40, POCKET MAP F9
4th Floor, 63 Las Vegas, 3716 Las Vegas Blvd S Ⓦ ocean-prime.com.

Ocean Prime's vast 400-seat Vegas restaurant plays the Vegas surf and turf game with finesse. Start with oysters on the half shell, sushi or a white truffle caviar devilled egg. Seafood mains include lobster linguine with roasted tomato butter. Prime steaks include a 16oz ribeye. Book ahead for space on the rooftop terrace. $$$

Picasso

MAP P.40, POCKET MAP F7
Bellagio, 3600 Las Vegas Blvd S
Ⓦ bellagio.com.

This elegant two-Michelin star restaurant has a beautiful view of the Bellagio fountains and original Picassos on its walls. Chef Julian Serrano offers a small selection of amazing French dishes that change seasonally, while the wine cellar is stocked with bottles from the finest European vineyards. $$$$

Scarpetta

MAP P.40, POCKET MAP K7
Level 3, The Cosmopolitan, 3708 Las Vegas

Blvd S ⓦ cosmopolitanlasvegas.com.
Courtesy of "new Italian" chef Scott
Conant, the food is even better
than the view at *Scarpetta,* which
has huge windows overlooking the
Bellagio fountains. All of Las Vegas
has flocked to enjoy starters like his
tuna "susci", and mains including
short rib and bone marrow
agnolotti (stuffed pasta). For the
full works, go for the tasting menu.
$$$

Bar and lounge

Chandelier

MAP P.40, POCKET MAP K6 & F9
Cosmopolitan, 3708 Las Vegas Blvd S
ⓦ cosmopolitanlasvegas.com.
Beneath the dazzling, dangling
canopy of the eponymous two-
million-crystal chandelier, the
Cosmopolitan's centrepiece bar
soars through three separate levels.
It's the middle floor where the
action is, with DJ music and a
buzzy crowd.

Clubs and music venues

The Chelsea

MAP P.40, POCKET MAP E9
Level 3, The Cosmopolitan, 3708 Las Vegas
Blvd S ⓦ cosmopolitanlasvegas.com.
Charge.
Targeted at The Cosmopolitan's
upscale clientele, The Chelsea is
entered via a grand staircase. The
venue sees a broad array of music
and comedy acts, from stalwarts
such as James Taylor and Smashing
Pumpkins to the modern icons of
Dua Lipa and Lizzo.

Dolby Live

MAP P.40, POCKET MAP B2
Park MGM, 3770 Las Vegas Blvd S
ⓦ parkmgm.com. See website for
schedule.
Five-thousand-seat indoor arena
formerly known as the Park Theater

and rebranded in 2021. Its stage,
which is larger than the Colosseum
at Caesars Palace, is primarily used
for live music. So far, it's hosted
residencies by the likes of Cher,
Stevie Wonder and Sting.

Marquee

MAP P.40, POCKET MAP F9 & K6
The Cosmopolitan, 3708 Las Vegas Blvd S
ⓦ marqueelasvegas.com. Charge.
This cutting-edge indoor-outdoor
nightclub with a pool-centred
"dayclub", features a 50ft-high
main floor, the Boombox,
overlooking the Strip, and the
Library, which has pool tables. The
dayclub is smaller than at Encore
(see page 67), but attracts bigger-
name DJs and celebrities. Add in
drinks and the dollars add up; buy
a wristband for the whole weekend.

T-Mobile Arena

MAP P.40, POCKET MAP A3
3780 Las Vegas Blvd S ⓦ t-mobilearena.
com. See website for schedule.
Set back from the Strip between
New York–New York and the
Park MGM, this huge, covered
stadium was unveiled in 2016
as the centrepiece of The Park
development. Holding twenty
thousand spectators, and home to
the Vegas Golden Knights hockey
team, it has put on gigs by Kanye
West, Justin Timberlake and
Metallica, plus boxing matches,
basketball games and award
ceremonies.

Show

O

MAP P.40, POCKET MAP E7
Bellagio, 3600 Las Vegas Blvd S
ⓦ cirquedusoleil.com.
This phenomenal show centres
on a metal-mesh stage, any part
of which can suddenly disappear
beneath the performers' feet. The
dazzling array of death-defying
leaps and plunges create a visual
spectacular you'll never forget.

The Central Strip

Long the scene of fierce inter-casino rivalries, the central portion of the Strip now feels much more like a pedestrian neighbourhood, where visitors stroll from one casino to the next thanks to new outdoor spaces like the Linq development adjoining the Flamingo and the Roman Plaza outside Caesars Palace. What's not obvious, however, is that all those casinos, from the block-spanning Caesars Palace to grizzled veterans like the Flamingo and Harrah's across the Strip, and newcomers like Paris and Planet Hollywood to the south, now belong to the same conglomerate – and you'd never guess it was Harrah's that came out on top.

Planet Hollywood

MAP P.50, POCKET MAP G9
3667 Las Vegas Blvd S Ⓦ caesars.com/
planet-hollywood.

The only Strip giant saddled with a brand name not otherwise known for gambling, **Planet Hollywood** has struggled to establish a strong identity; it's not part of the dining chain or even an independent entity. The building itself opened in 2000 as a new version of the long-established Aladdin, where Elvis Presley married Priscilla in 1966. Planet Hollywood took it over in 2004, after the Aladdin went broke in the wake of 9/11, but they in turn soon floundered and sold out to Harrah's in 2010.

Planet Hollywood subsequently raised its profile by signing Britney Spears for a long-term residency, which ended in 2017. As the Aladdin, though, it always seemed to be empty, thanks to the design flaw that meant the door from the Strip was too hard to find – simply rectified by erecting a huge sign reading "Casino Entrance". The main attraction within is the **Miracle Mile** mall (see page 48); the actual casino is relatively small, and is largely targeted, with its blaring music and flashing lights, at hip young visitors.

Miracle Mile

MAP P.50, POCKET MAP G8
Planet Hollywood, 3663 Las Vegas Blvd S
Ⓦ miraclemileshopslv.com.

Coiled like an enormous snake around and through Planet Hollywood, the **Miracle Mile** mall is nonetheless an entirely separate operation. Built at the same time as the new Aladdin, in 2000, and still bearing traces of its original Arabian Nights theming, it was credited by some as being responsible for the Aladdin's financial failure; given the chance to stroll into a mall without having to walk through a casino en route, Strip sightseers simply ignored the Aladdin altogether. Besides a free **"rainstorm" attraction** that runs on weekends, the Miracle Mile holds a wide range of bars, restaurants and theatres to complement the clothing boutiques, shoe shops and galleries (see page 56).

Paris

MAP P.50, POCKET MAP G8
3655 Las Vegas Blvd S Ⓦ caesars.com/
paris-las-vegas.

Designed by the architects previously responsible for New York–New York, and opened a few months before the millennium, **Paris** represented the final flourish of the Las Vegas craze for building entire miniature cities. Its exterior remains one of the Strip's most enjoyable spectacles, surmounted by a gigantic Eiffel Tower whose legs crash through the ceiling into the heart of the casino itself, and anchored by the Arc de Triomphe, the Opera and a Montgolfier hot-air balloon, which becomes a glowing landmark at night.

Although it's slightly misleading to think of Paris as a separate casino at all – it was originally built as an extension to sister hotel Bally's, now named Horseshoe (see page 51), to which it's linked by a broad corridor at the back of the building – it was an immediate hit. With both of these properties now owned by Caesars Entertainment, the tail these days is clearly wagging the dog, and Horseshoe feels like a minor adjunct to Paris. In 2023, Horseshoe's Jubilee Tower was moved under the Paris umbrella, diminishing it further.

Pleasing Parisian touches, such as the ironwork that echoes the city's Metro stations, still abound throughout the interior. From the excellent **creperie** to the pastry shops and bridal-wear boutiques, the great majority of Paris's shops, restaurants and bars have some sort of French connection. Much of it is tongue-in-cheek, so even the more tenuous links, as in calling the sports bar the **Le Bar du Sport**, are just part of the fun. The one area where visitors have balked at the Gallic flavour has been entertainment; Paris has long since abandoned its hopes of staging all-French productions (like, say, *Phantom of the Opera* or *Les Miserables*) in favour of safer options like the musical *Marilyn* or *I love the '90s* show.

Eiffel Tower Experience

MAP P.50, POCKET MAP G8
Paris, 3655 Las Vegas Blvd S Ⓦ caesars.com/paris-las-vegas. Charge.
Towering 540ft over the Strip, Las Vegas's version of the **Eiffel Tower** is half the height of the Seine-side original. It's not simply a half-sized replica, however; if it was, you wouldn't be able to squeeze into the elevators, for example. In addition, this one is made of steel not iron,

Paris

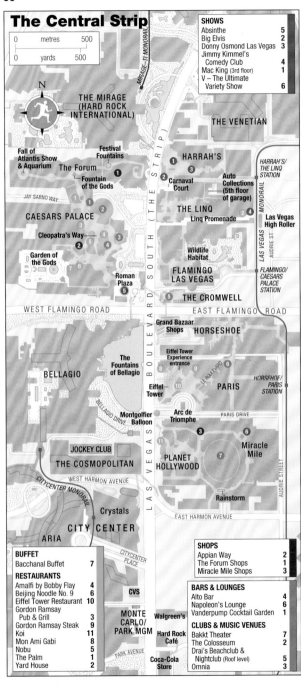

The Central Strip

| metres | 500 |
| yards | 500 |

THE MIRAGE (HARD ROCK INTERNATIONAL)

THE VENETIAN

Fall of Atlantis Show & Aquarium

Festival Fountains

HARRAH'S

The Forum

Fountain of the Gods

HARRAH'S/ THE LINQ STATION

JAY SARNO WAY

Carnaval Court

Auto Collections (5th floor of garage)

CAESARS PALACE

THE LINQ

Linq Promenade

Las Vegas High Roller

Cleopatra's Way

Garden of the Gods

Wildlife Habitat

FLAMINGO/ CAESARS PALACE STATION

Roman Plaza

FLAMINGO LAS VEGAS

THE CROMWELL

WEST FLAMINGO ROAD

EAST FLAMINGO ROAD

Grand Bazaar Shops

HORSESHOE

BELLAGIO

The Fountains of Bellagio

Eiffel Tower Experience entrance

Eiffel Tower

LE BOULEVARD

PARIS

HORSESHOE/ PARIS STATION

Montgolfier Balloon

Arc de Triomphe

PARIS DRIVE

JOCKEY CLUB

THE COSMOPOLITAN

PLANET HOLLYWOOD

Miracle Mile

AUDRIE STREET

WEST HARMON AVENUE

CITYCENTER MONORAIL

Crystals

Rainstorm

CITY CENTER

EAST HARMON AVENUE

ARIA

CITYCENTER PLACE

CVS

MONTE CARLO/ PARK MGM

Walgreens

PARK AVENUE

Hard Rock Café

Coca-Cola Store

SHOWS

Absinthe	5
Big Elvis	2
Donny Osmond Las Vegas	3
Jimmy Kimmel's Comedy Club	4
Mac King (3rd floor)	1
V – The Ultimate Variety Show	6

BUFFET

Bacchanal Buffet	7

RESTAURANTS

Amalfi by Bobby Flay	4
Beijing Noodle No. 9	6
Eiffel Tower Restaurant	10
Gordon Ramsay Pub & Grill	3
Gordon Ramsay Steak	9
Koi	11
Mon Ami Gabi	8
Nobu	5
The Palm	1
Yard House	2

SHOPS

Appian Way	2
The Forum Shops	1
Miracle Mile Shops	3

BARS & LOUNGES

Alto Bar	4
Napoleon's Lounge	6
Vanderpump Cocktail Garden	1

CLUBS & MUSIC VENUES

Bakkt Theater	7
The Colosseum	2
Drai's Beachclub & Nightclub (Roof level)	5
Omnia	3

and doesn't have a public staircase to the top.

Visitors can either dine in the luxury restaurant 100ft up, or buy a ticket inside Paris's main entrance for the **Eiffel Tower Experience** and ride all the way to the summit viewing platform. The prime time to come is at sunset, although it opens late into the evening when the bright lights take over; its builders always cheekily intended the Eiffel Tower to be a perfect vantage point for watching the Bellagio fountains.

Horseshoe

MAP P.50, POCKET MAP G7
3645 Las Vegas Blvd S Ⓦ caesars.com/horseshoe-las-vegas.

These days, you could easily fail to notice **Horseshoe** (named **Bally's up until 2022**), set well back from the Strip opposite Bellagio. When it opened in 1973, however, this was the MGM Grand, the biggest hotel in the world. Only after a terrible hotel fire killed 84 people here in 1980 was it bought and renamed by the gaming manufacturer Bally's, and a new MGM Grand constructed further south. Now owned by Caesars Entertainment, Horseshoe became a humdrum casino with many attempts made to revivify the property.

Horseshoe was built in the era when casinos still needed huge Strip-front car parks. Legendary in Las Vegas lore as the landing site for Nicolas Cage and the parachuting Elvises in the 1992 movie *Honeymoon in Vegas*, and subsequently spanned by a network of neon-covered walkways, the former Horseshoe car park has now at last been built over to become the site of an open-air mall, the **Grand Bazaar Shops**. The small booths and kiosks are largely devoted to snacks and souvenirs, so it's hardly a must-see attraction, but it's another step towards making the Strip more pedestrian-friendly.

Rod Stewart at The Colosseum

Caesars Palace

MAP P.50, POCKET MAP F6
3570 Las Vegas Blvd S
Ⓦ caesarspalace.com.

Still a Las Vegas headliner in its own right, fifty years since it was built, **Caesars Palace** remains arguably the biggest name on the Strip. During the casino-building spree either side of the millennium, it slipped for a moment behind its newer rivals, to the point where Harrah's Entertainment were able to buy up control. Recognizing the prestige value of the name, however, they've not only reinvigorated Caesars and put it back on top, but changed their own name to Caesars Entertainment.

Caesars Palace was originally the creation of **Jay Sarno**, a hard-gambling associate of legendary Teamsters leader Jimmy Hoffa. Cobbled together for just $24 million, it was unveiled in 1966, complete with clerks dressed as Roman centurions and cocktail waitresses kitted out like Cleopatra. Sarno himself doubled his money and sold out in 1969; he moved on to build Circus Circus, and eventually died of a heart attack in a suite at Caesars in 1984.

As well as coming up with the Caesars Palace name, designed to appeal to American and European gamblers alike, Sarno also decreed that the one thing it will never have is an apostrophe – it does not belong to Caesar, it's filled by the thousands of Caesars who choose to visit it. His crucial legacy, however, was that he'd set Caesars up on an expanse of land – originally rented from Kirk Kerkorian, who remained a major Las Vegas player until his death in 2015 – that has so far proved big enough to hold every enlargement architects have been able to imagine.

Pausing to admire Caesars Palace from the Strip is one of the great joys of visiting Las Vegas. White marble Classical statues are everywhere you look, from Julius Caesar forever hailing a cab on the main driveway to the Winged Victory of Samothrace guarding a row of gently cascading pools. Most impressive of all are the ornate fountains that surround the entrance to the Forum mall.

The central bulk of Caesars Palace is still proudly set back around 150 yards from the Strip; all that space between the casino and the Strip originally held an enormous car park. Once Las Vegas visitors began to arrive by plane instead of by car, the gap became a deterrent to pedestrians. It was Caesars that pioneered the use of long moving walkways to haul them in – and naturally neglected to build corresponding outbound walkways to let them back out again. Bit by bit, the space has been built over. First, at the northern end, the vast **Forum** mall (see opposite) steadily extended until it reached all the way to the Strip; then the mighty **Colosseum** appeared alongside, in 2003; and more recently the **Roman Plaza** has burgeoned at the south, and now holds bars, restaurants and even, currently, a circus marquee, which is home to the *Absinthe* show (see page 60).

Inside, Caesars Palace bewilders most first-time visitors. Unlike newer Las Vegas properties, designed to be user-friendly and let you find what you're looking for, Caesars was laid out in the hope that gamblers might never be able to escape.

Making your way between the casino itself and the Forum is easy enough; the two simply meet on the casino floor. However, exploring the rest of Caesars Palace is less straightforward. A network of narrow and circuitous corridors lead to the older **Appian Way** mall, which offers the chance of a close-up inspection, from directly below, of Michelangelo's naked *David*, and Cleopatra's Way, home to the Egyptian-themed *Cleopatra's Barge* nightclub (see page 58).

Much of the rest of the property, including the luxurious **Garden of the Gods** pool complex, based on

The Buffet of Buffets

Although buffets have been one of the slowest Vegas experiences to bounce back after Covid, buffet fans should watch out for the **Buffet of Buffets pass**. They are sold at the buffets in every Caesars-owned casino, which allows 24-hour unrestricted access to them all. Use it to eat at, say, 8pm one night, 7pm the next, and you get two dinners into the bargain. Note, however, that each visit to the buffets at Rio, and *Bacchanal Buffet* at Caesars Palace, costs extra. Four years after the start of Covid, some of the buffets were yet to reopen.

The Cromwell

the baths of Pompeii, is only open to registered guests.

The Forum

MAP P.50, POCKET MAP F5
3500 Las Vegas Blvd S Ⓦ simon.com/mall.
By opening the **Forum** mall in 1992, Caesars Palace not only became the first Strip casino to turn both shopping and dining into major reasons to visit Las Vegas, it also created one of the city's most iconic attractions.

Though widely copied ever since, the Forum's domed false-sky ceiling still packs a mind-blowing punch. Designed to evoke the skyline of ancient Rome, it cycles hourly between the dazzling blue of "day" and the orange glow of "night".

Sadly, though, many of the kitschier elements of the Forum's earlier years, such as the animatronic "living statues" that adorned its centrepiece fountains, have been discarded in favour of ever more opulent and ornate decor. The most striking feature these days is the amazing convoluted spiral escalator at the Forum's main Strip entrance. Its separate moving pathways follow different trajectories, so you can never be sure they'll take you where you want to go.

The **Forum Shops** themselves still rank as Las Vegas's premier shopping spot (see page 56).

The Cromwell

MAP P.50, POCKET MAP G7
3595 Las Vegas Blvd S Ⓦ caesars.com/cromwell.
Squeezed into a sandwich-sized slot at one of Las Vegas's prime intersections, the Strip's smallest casino used to be a budget alternative, known originally as the Barbary Coast and since 2007 as Bill's Gamblin' Hall & Saloon. It reopened in 2014, however, as a self-styled "boutique hotel", **The Cromwell**.

For no obvious reason, the name is intended to evoke Parisian splendour rather than those titans of English history, Thomas and Oliver. Its 188 rooms are now luxurious and expensive, while the principal new features are **Giada**, an Italian restaurant run by TV chef Giada de Laurentiis, and **Drai's** (see page 59), a massive indoor-outdoor rooftop club; the entire structure had to be strengthened to support the colossal weight of its various pools and pavilions.

Flamingo Las Vegas

MAP P.50, POCKET MAP G6
3555 Las Vegas Blvd S Ⓦ caesars.com/flamingo-las-vegas.

Now that it's just another glossy casino, shoulder to shoulder in the Strip's endless procession of identikit giants, it's all but impossible to picture **the Flamingo** in its original form. Whatever anyone may tell you, when it opened in 1946 it wasn't the very first Strip resort of them all. Standing alone in the desert, however, a mile south of its nearest neighbour, the Last Frontier, the Flamingo was an enticing hundred-room oasis that put Las Vegas on the map as a glamorous, even dangerous, getaway.

Not that the Flamingo was an immediate hit. So disastrously over-budget that it was forced to close within a fortnight, its initial failure cost owner Benjamin "Bugsy" Siegel his life, when his fellow mobsters gunned him down the next year. By then, however, the Flamingo was already going strong, and a wave of imitators was starting to appear.

With Bugsy a distant, sanitized memory, the Flamingo these days is much more Donny and Marie – until Covid, long-term residents in its showroom – than Don Corleone. Its current owners, Caesars Entertainment, target it largely at older visitors who remember Las Vegas as it used to be back in the 1980s, when the Flamingo was still the biggest hotel in the world, and before everything had to keep reinventing itself to suit the latest trend.

From its superb neon sign and the Strip-facing patio of *Jimmy Buffett's Margaritaville* at the front, to the real-life flamingos and penguins in the free **Wildlife Habitat** and garden-set pool complex around the back, there's a lot to like about the Flamingo. As The Linq development next door expanded, The Linq Promenade was born – a dining, shopping and entertainment district complete with a 550ft observation wheel, located between The Linq Hotel and Flamingo.

The Linq

MAP P.50, POCKET MAP G5
3535 Las Vegas Blvd S Ⓦ caesars.com/linq.

Caesars Entertainment responded to MGM Resorts' construction of CityCenter by carving out its own rival "neighbourhood". Centring on the showpiece High Roller, it took what was previously a narrow roadway between the Flamingo and Imperial Palace casinos, and turned it into a broader pedestrian corridor of shops, bars and restaurants.

The long-standing Imperial Palace was not demolished, but totally "re-skinned", with its previous Japanese facade stripped away and its interior decor transformed. Briefly re-christened the Quad, it has now appropriated the name of the entire project – **The Linq**.

Flamingo

The High Roller

New features include a 32-lane bowling alley with its own restaurant, plus a tattoo studio, a Harley-Davidson clothing shop, and several bars.

High Roller

MAP P.50, POCKET MAP H6
3545 Las Vegas Blvd S Ⓦ caesars.com/linq. Charge.

The world's second largest observation wheel, the **High Roller** stands just off the Strip at the far end of the pedestrianized Linq entertainment district. At 550ft, it's over a hundred feet taller than the 443ft London Eye and rotates non-stop. Each of its 28 see-through cabins can carry up to forty passengers. The long-range panoramas are spectacular, though intervening buildings mean it doesn't offer ground-level views of the Strip.

Harrah's

MAP P.50, POCKET MAP G5
3475 Las Vegas Blvd S Ⓦ caesars.com/harrahs-las-vegas.

Harrah's is the great unsung success story of the Strip. When all its rivals were going crazy for adding eye-catching, child-friendly gimmicks, constructing replica cities and enticing young revellers to day-night pool parties, Harrah's just carried on giving parents the same old, same old formula of cheap eats, plentiful slots and middle-of-the-road entertainment. And it did it all so well that one by one Harrah's swallowed up all of its Central Strip rivals. Then, having bought the lot, the Harrah's organization simply changed its name to Caesars Entertainment; it's as if it never happened.

For anyone under a certain age, Harrah's itself remains as middle America as ever. Walk past on the Strip, and your attention may be captured by the performers on the open-air **Carnaval Court** stage, but step inside and you're in a soporific time warp, where a celebrity chef superstar's eponymous *Ramsay's Kitchen* is the biggest attraction. To be fair, Harrah's does put on some good-value daytime shows, including *Mac King* (see page 61) and *Big Elvis* (see page 60), but it's no place for thrill-seeking sightseers.

Shops

Appian Way

MAP P.50, POCKET MAP F6
Caesars Palace, 3570 Las Vegas Blvd S
Ⓦ caesars.com/caesars-palace.

Much smaller than the Forum, the **Appian Way** is arrayed along two corridors just off the casino floor at Caesars Palace. Centring on an 18ft marble replica of Michelangelo's *David*, it includes upscale jewellery stores, clothing at Misura, and a shop selling Caesars' merchandise.

The Forum Shops

MAP P.50, POCKET MAP F5
3500 Las Vegas Blvd S Ⓦ simon.com/mall.

Still going strong after a quarter of a century, The Forum Shops is foot-for-foot the country's most successful mall. That's partly because its big-name brands tend to be squeezed into smaller spaces than usual. While its two main "streets" are hardly full of surprises – expect to see an Apple Store, Nike and H&M, for example – they do offer a very intense burst of shopping.

Miracle Mile Shops

Miracle Mile Shops

MAP P.50, POCKET MAP G8
Planet Hollywood, 3663 Las Vegas Blvd S
Ⓦ miraclemileshopslv.com.

Give or take the odd fountain, the largest casino mall, the Miracle Mile Shops, could be just about anywhere. Easily entered straight from the Strip, it really is a mile long; walk from one end to the other and you'll pass a huge range of stores, from mall staples like Foot Locker, lululemon, Sephora and Billabong to some jaw-droppingly awful "art galleries" and a couple of ABC convenience stores.

Buffet

Bacchanal Buffet

MAP P.50, POCKET MAP F6
Caesars Palace, 3570 Las Vegas Blvd S
Ⓦ caesars.com/caesars-palace.

Las Vegas's top-ranked gourmet buffet – the best at any Caesars-owned property – revolutionized the buffet concept. It features over 250 freshly made items daily, from sushi, dim sum and pho soup to fresh oysters and wood-fired pizzas,

prepared by chefs at nine separate "show kitchens". $$$

Restaurants

Amalfi by Bobby Flay

MAP P.50, POCKET MAP F6
Caesars Palace, 3570 Las Vegas Blvd S
Ⓦ caesars.com/caesars-palace.
Bobby Flay's famous Mesa Grill restaurant at Caesars Palace won him, and then lost him, his Michelin star soon after opening in 2004. But during Covid 2021, the restaurant was reimagined as a seafood eatery inspired by the Amalfi coastline, south of Naples in Italy. Wares are displayed on ice within, and you can chat to the in-house fishmonger before buying. Indicative of the light, fresh flavours here is the squid ink fettucine, with lobster and shrimp. $$$

Beijing Noodle No. 9

MAP P.50, POCKET MAP F6
Caesars Palace, 3570 Las Vegas Blvd S
Ⓦ caesars.com/caesars-palace.
Approached via aquariums that hold a thousand goldfish and resembling a pale, mysterious, underwater cavern, this Chinese noodle shop is one of Las Vegas's most enjoyable places to eat. Fortunately, the food matches the setting, though with dim sum buns and dumplings, and (large) noodle dishes. $$

Eiffel Tower Restaurant

MAP P.50, POCKET MAP G8
Paris, 3655 Las Vegas Blvd S Ⓦ caesars.com/paris-las-vegas.
Undoubtedly one of the finest views available to diners in Las Vegas is found 100ft in the air, partway up the Eiffel Tower at Paris. The plate glass window looks out over the Fountain of Bellagio and surrounding Strip. If you're breaking the bank, start at the caviar bar, with Imperial Golden Osetra Caviar, one of the finest available, on the menu. Mains range from filet mignon to chicken breast with parsnip puree. $$$$

Gordon Ramsay Pub & Grill

MAP P.50, POCKET MAP F6
Caesars Palace, 3570 Las Vegas Blvd S
Ⓦ caesars.com/caesars-palace.
Stylized version of a British pub, run by TV chef and Las Vegas darling Gordon Ramsay, with some tables adjoining the casino floor and the rest inside, close to a bar decked out with pretend red phone kiosks. Expect dishes such as fish and chips, or roasted beef Wellington, along with 36 draught beers, best enjoyed during the "Hell's Kitchen" Happy Hour on weekday afternoons. $$$

Gordon Ramsay Steak

MAP P.50, POCKET MAP G7
Paris, 3655 Las Vegas Blvd S
Ⓦ caesars.com/paris-las-vegas.
For his first Las Vegas venture, perfectionist pottymouth Gordon Ramsay played it safe, opening a high-class steakhouse near Paris's main entrance – its tunnel approach represents the trip from France to England, incidentally. Diners select from a trolley laden with marbled, aged slabs of prime meat; you'll find a superbly cooked veal chop or American Wagyu fillet here, otherwise the tasting menu includes Beef Wellington. $$$

Koi

MAP P.50, POCKET MAP G8
Planet Hollywood, 3667 Las Vegas Blvd S
Ⓦ koirestaurant.com.
While not the celebrity favourite it is in Hollywood, this fancy restaurant serves tasty Japanese food at what, for Las Vegas, are reasonable prices – especially considering its views of Bellagio's fountains. Sushi rolls, tuna tartare or tempura shrimp precede mains such as steamed sea bass or wasabi short ribs. $$$

Mon Ami Gabi

MAP P.50, POCKET MAP G7
Paris, 3655 Las Vegas Blvd S
Ⓦ monamigabi.com.

Among the first Las Vegas restaurants to offer al fresco dining, this exuberant evocation of a Paris pavement brasserie remains the city's premier lunchtime pick. The terrace tables go quickly, but are among the best for people-watching in Vegas. For a real taste of France, you can't beat a *croque-madame* (ham, cheese and egg sandwich) for breakfast; *moules frites* (mussels and chips) for lunch; or *steak frites* for dinner. $$$

Nobu

MAP P.50, POCKET MAP F6
Caesars Palace, 3570 Las Vegas Blvd S
Ⓦ caesars.com.

Flagship restaurant for the world-spanning empire of Japanese-Peruvian chef Nobu Matsuhisa, whose fans are so devoted that Caesars even has its own Nobu hotel tower into the bargain. Ambience and audience alike are very upmarket; and the food is exquisite, with hot mains including black cod miso or beef tenderloin, and a full chef's-choice tasting menu. $$$$

The Palm

MAP P.50, POCKET MAP F5
Forum Shops, Caesars Palace, 3500 Las Vegas Blvd S Ⓦ thepalm.com.

A veteran of the Forum scene, this offshoot of the legendary New York steakhouse offers a stylish, surprisingly formal escape from the shopping mania outside. For lunch, there are salads, burgers or sandwiches. In the evening, highlights include classic Italian veal dishes and the prime, 24oz rib-eye steak. $$$

Yard House

MAP P.50, POCKET MAP H5
Linq Promenade, 3545 Las Vegas Blvd S
Ⓦ yardhouse.com.

Lively restaurant/bar along the pedestrian mall that leads to the High Roller, where the extensive food menu ranges from jambalaya or Southern fried chicken to a vegetarian quinoa salad. They also offer craft ales and ciders from around the world, many of which you can indeed drink from a genuine "yard". $$

Bars and lounges

Alto Bar

MAP P.50, POCKET MAP F6
Caesars Palace, 3570 Las Vegas Blvd S
Ⓦ caesars.com/caesars-palace.

Catch your breath after walking Caesars' endless hallways in this up-to-the-minute open-fronted lounge, which replaced the much-missed Seahorse Lounge in 2016. Raised above the casino floor, and specializing in very fancy cocktails, it's the perfect spot to see and be seen, though you can also hide away in a private booth.

Napoleon's Lounge

MAP P.50, POCKET MAP H7
Paris, 3655 Las Vegas Blvd S Ⓦ caesars.com/paris-las-vegas.

Come in the early evening to this plush, dimly lit, bordello-red bar, poised halfway along the internal corridor that connects Paris to Horseshoe. While there may be a lounge act on stage, like a vocal group or comedian, it still feels like a sophisticated venue at which to enjoy a glass of champagne, cognac, cocktails or cigars. Between 9pm and 1am nightly, however, things turn much more raucous, as duelling pianists vie to belt out whatever tunes the audience requests (and is prepared to tip for) – expect there to be energetic, enthusiastic sing-along renditions of *Bohemian Rhapsody* and the like.

Vanderpump Cocktail Garden

MAP P.50, POCKET MAP F5

Mariah Carey at The Colosseum

Caesars Palace, 3570 Las Vegas Blvd S
Ⓦ caesars.com.
Celebrity restaurateur and *Real
Housewives of Beverly Hills* star
Lisa Vanderpump opened this,
her first Las Vegas venture, in
2019. The interior features Nick
Alain lighting via wall panels and
a ceiling dome, which provides
an evolving ambience throughout
the day. A sylvan forest theme
adds another touch of class to the
bespoke, hand-crafted cocktails,
which play on both Vanderpump's
celebrity and the Caesars theme,
such as the Please her, Caesar! with
rosé Champagne, elderflower and
vodka.

Clubs and music venues

Bakkt Theater
MAP P.50, POCKET MAP H1
Planet Hollywood, 3667 Las Vegas Blvd S
Ⓦ caesars.com/planet-hollywood. Check
website for schedule.
Originally the Aladdin Theater and
cycling through six more names
since 2006, Bakkt Theatre is the
centrepiece entertainment spot
at Planet Hollywood. The space
has hosted a number of notable
musicians on long-term residencies,
including Britney Spears, Gwen
Stefani, Backstreet Boys and Kelly
Clarkson.

The Colosseum
MAP P.50, POCKET MAP F5
Caesars Palace, 3570 Las Vegas Blvd S
Ⓦ thecolosseum.com. Check website for
schedule.
Built in 2003 to house a long-term
residency by Celine Dion, the
4000-seat Colosseum is one of the
last great strongholds of the old-
style Las Vegas headliner. Celine
still returns frequently, while Adele
performed throughout 2023. Other
notable stars who have played more
than 100 shows here include Elton
John, Bette Midler, Cher and Rod
Stewart.

Drai's Beachclub & Nightclub
MAP P.50, POCKET MAP G7
The Cromwell, 3595 Las Vegas Blvd S
Ⓦ caesars.com. Charge.
This huge indoor-outdoor night/
day club, on The Cromwell's

THE CENTRAL STRIP

roof, enjoys the best Strip views. Named for EDM entrepreneur and film producer Victor Drai, previously responsible for creating XS at Encore and Tryst at Wynn Las Vegas, it has big-name DJs and live performers – plus go-go dancers, with poolside cabanas for high-rollers.

Omnia

MAP P.50, POCKET MAP F6
Caesars Palace, 3570 Las Vegas Blvd S
ⓦ caesars.com. Charge.
Unveiled in 2015 as the successor to the massively popular Pure, this club boasts a huge open-air Strip-view terrace. Ordinary mortals can expect a long queue, and astonishing prices for drinks for what is truly a once-in-a-lifetime Las Vegas experience, with the world's biggest DJs.

Shows

Absinthe

MAP P.50, POCKET MAP F6
Caesars Palace, 3570 Las Vegas Blvd S
ⓦ caesars.com. Charge.

Absinthe

Staged in the round, in a marquee on Caesars' outdoor Roman Plaza, this no-holds-barred circus-tinged burlesque show has taken Las Vegas by storm. Conceived as a crude and abrasive counterpoint to the fey whimsy of Cirque du Soleil, and eschewing PC in all its forms, it's more of a drunken night out than a traditional show, but it still charges Cirque-level prices.

Big Elvis

MAP P.50, POCKET MAP G5
Piano Bar, Harrah's, 3475 Las Vegas Blvd S
ⓦ caesars.com/harrahs-las-vegas. Free.
Las Vegas's biggest and best-loved Elvis impersonator, Pete Vallee, has shucked off the pounds in the last few years to become merely Large Elvis. His King-like voice still packs a powerful punch, though, and his mastery of Elvis's repertoire and easy audience rapport – requests welcome – make this the best free show in town.

Donny Osmond Las Vegas

MAP P.50, POCKET MAP G5
Harrah's, 3475 Las Vegas Blvd S
ⓦ mackingshow.com. Charge.

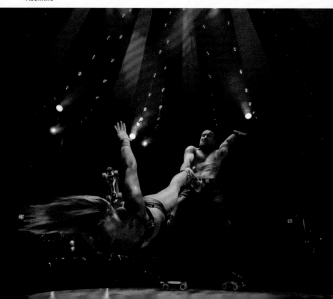

Donny Osmond

Moving on from an 11-year show with sister Marie Osmond at the Flamingo, Donny debuted his solo show at Harrah's in 2021. A live band, sequined dancers and dynamic choreography bring the energy to the parade of hits from his numerous records, which have garnered the singer dozens of gold records.

Jimmy Kimmel's Comedy Club

MAP P.50, POCKET MAP H5
The Linq, 3535 Las Vegas Blvd S
Ⓦ jimmykimmelscomedyclub.com. Charge.
Las Vegas has long been known for locking top comedians into long term residencies, and Jimmy Kimmel's continues the trend. This specialized venue hosts touring household names and regular performers. The latter group includes Jill Kimmel (Jimmy's sister), *America's Got Talent* finalist Gina Brillon, and comedy magician Farrell Dillon.

Mac King

MAP P.50, POCKET MAP G5
Harrah's, 3475 Las Vegas Blvd S
Ⓦ mackingshow.com. Charge.
Just so there's no doubt, Mac King is billed as a comedy magician. With his clownish country-boy persona, clean-talking patter, easy way with his audience and family-friendly prices – plus of course his stunning sleight of hand – he's Las Vegas's best daytime entertainment bargain.

V – The Ultimate Variety Show

MAP P.50, POCKET MAP H8
Miracle Mile, Planet Hollywood, 3663 Las Vegas Blvd S Ⓦ vtheshow.com. Charge.
This enjoyable, long-running variety show features established acts and crowd-pleasing routines. Regulars include "hip-hop contortionist" Turf; gloriously deadpan Mexican juggler Wally Eastwood; and Russ Merlin, whose Halloween mask audience-volunteer stunt brings the house down.

The North Strip

Along the North Strip a vibrant cluster of high-end properties compete to grab visitors' attention with gimmicks like the forthcoming guitar-shaped hotel (Hard Rock International), Renaissance bridges (the Venetian) and all-round gilded opulence (Wynn Las Vegas). This part of the Strip was where things used to get personal, with fiercely competitive tycoons Sheldon Adelson, former owner of the Venetian and the Palazzo, locked in fierce rivalry with Steve Wynn, former owner of the similarly twinned Wynn Las Vegas and Encore, up until the latter was accused of sexual misconduct in 2018, and the former's death in 2021. The Venetian and Palazzo were subsequently bought out by private equity firm Apollo Global Management and the inter-hotel rivalry fizzled out. The North Strip was regarded as stretching almost all the way to downtown until the recession, when many of the veteran casinos that lay further north were closed down, and most of the projects scheduled to replace them abandoned. After years of empty lots, change is afoot at this end of the Strip, as investors return in droves. Shiny new façades abound, suggesting that the Strip's newest casinos are opting for Wynn-style opulence over Adelson-style whimsy.

The Mirage

MAP P.64, POCKET MAP F4
3400 Las Vegas Blvd S Ⓦ mirage.com.
Unveiled as entrepreneur Steve Wynn's first Strip venture, in 1989 – when Las Vegas seemed to be in decline, and no new Strip hotels had been built for sixteen years – the **Mirage** can justly claim to have changed the city overnight. Proving that by investing in luxury, glamour and spectacle, casinos could bring back the crowds, it spawned such a host of imitators that now, ironically, it no longer stands out from the pack.

Perhaps even more ironically, the Mirage entered a decline that, at the time of research, appeared highly likely to spell the end for the hotel. Plans include remodelling and replacing it with a new Hard Rock International hotel – with work likely to begin either at the end of 2023 or in early 2024 – and removing the iconic **volcano** – which erupts nightly and is one of the Strip's great free spectacles – to replace it with a giant guitar-shaped hotel tower, holding up to 600 rooms. The Mirage Towers will remain open during this process. The **Secret Garden and Dolphin Habitat** closed in 2022.

TI (Treasure Island)

MAP P.64, POCKET MAP G3
3300 Las Vegas Blvd S
Ⓦ treasureisland.com.
TI (Treasure Island) was built in 1993 as a sort of kid brother to the Mirage (see page 62) next door, with an all-pervasive pirate theme aimed at family visitors.

While it's still physically connected to the Mirage by a free **monorail**, it's now under separate ownership, and distances itself from its yo-ho-ho past by using the anodyne acronym TI.

The most prominent feature of Treasure Island during its first twenty years was the shallow **lagoon** in front, home to twin replica pirate ships that were crewed first by battling buccaneers and then later by gyrating, bikini-clad "sirens" whose after-dark music-and-dance shows lured in vast crowds. Architectural theorists tied themselves in knots arguing whether Treasure Island was a building, a performance space or a theme park. Ships and sirens alike have now gone, prosaically replaced by a crass Mexican "party restaurant", *Señor Frog's*, and a huge CVS grocery/pharmacy.

Phil Ruffin, former owner of the now-vanished New Frontier, bought TI in 2008, when MGM Resorts ran short of cash to build CityCenter. He's steadily turning it into a blue-collar joint, home to nightspots like *Gilley's Saloon* (see page 74), though he's hung on to Cirque's first-ever Las Vegas show, *Mystère* (see page 76).

The Venetian

MAP P.64, POCKET MAP G4
3355 Las Vegas Blvd S Ⓦ venetian.com.

The hugely successful **Venetian** casino opened in 1999 on the site of the much-mourned Sands, the former Las Vegas home of Frank Sinatra and the Rat Pack. Former owner, Sheldon Adelson, may have lacked the design flair of Steve Wynn, but he had an unarguable genius for making money. After buying the Sands in 1988, he amassed a billion-dollar fortune from the annual tech-industry trade show COMDEX. The casino – which came under the ownership of private equity firm Apollo Global Management in 2021 following Adelson's death – remains one of the most popular hotels on the Strip.

The Venetian itself is a re-creation of the ultimate honeymoon photo album; Adelson returned from his 1991 honeymoon trip to Venice with the idea of building a vast replica of the city. Around a dozen distinct Venetian landmarks squeeze side by side into the casino's Strip facade, while its main entrance lies between two columns, modelled on a pair brought to Venice's Piazza San Marco from Constantinople in 1172. One is topped by St Theodore, the

The Grand Canal at The Venetian

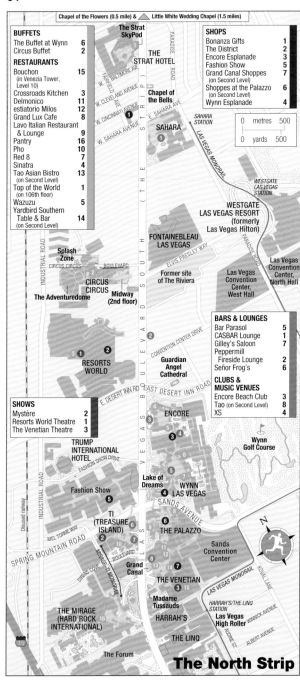

Chapel of the Flowers (0.5 mile) & Little White Wedding Chapel (1.5 miles)

BUFFETS
The Buffet at Wynn 6
Circus Buffet 2

RESTAURANTS
Bouchon 15
(in Venezia Tower, Level 10)
Crossroads Kitchen 3
Delmonico 11
estiatorio Milos 12
Grand Lux Cafe 8
Lavo Italian Restaurant & Lounge 9
Pantry 16
Pho 10
Red 8 7
Sinatra 4
Tao Asian Bistro 13
(on Second Level)
Top of the World 1
(on 106th floor)
Wazuzu 5
Yardbird Southern Table & Bar 14
(on Second Level)

SHOPS
Bonanza Gifts 1
The District 2
Encore Esplanade 3
Fashion Show 5
Grand Canal Shoppes 7
(on Second Level)
Shoppes at the Palazzo 6
(on Second Level)
Wynn Esplanade 4

0 metres 500
0 yards 500

SHOWS
Mystère 2
Resorts World Theatre 1
The Venetian Theatre 3

BARS & LOUNGES
Bar Parasol 5
CASBAR Lounge 1
Gilley's Saloon 7
Peppermill Fireside Lounge 2
Señor Frog's 6

CLUBS & MUSIC VENUES
Encore Beach Club 3
Tao (on Second Level) 8
XS 4

The Strat SkyPod
THE STRAT HOTEL
Chapel of the Bells
SAHARA STATION
SAHARA
W. BALTIMORE AVE.
W. CLEVELAND AVENUE
W. CINCINNATI AVENUE
E. SAHARA AVE.
W. SAHARA AVENUE
FAIRFIELD AVE.
PARADISE ROAD
LAS VEGAS MONORAIL
WESTGATE LAS VEGAS STATION
WESTGATE LAS VEGAS RESORT (formerly Las Vegas Hilton)
FONTAINEBLEAU LAS VEGAS
ELVIS PRESLEY WAY
Former site of The Riviera
Las Vegas Convention Center, West Hall
Las Vegas Convention Center, North Hall
Splash Zone
CIRCUS CIRCUS
The Adventuredome
Midway (2nd floor)
INDUSTRIAL ROAD
BOULEVARD
RESORTS WORLD
CONVENTION CENTER DRIVE
E. DESERT INN RD. EAST DESERT INN ROAD
Guardian Angel Cathedral
ENCORE
Wynn Golf Course
TRUMP INTERNATIONAL HOTEL
FASHION SHOW DRIVE
Fashion Show
Lake of Dreams
WYNN LAS VEGAS
SANDS AVENUE
TI (TREASURE ISLAND)
THE PALAZZO
Sands Convention Center
SPRING MOUNTAIN ROAD
MEL TORMÉ WAY
Disused railway
Industrial Road
SIEGFRIED & ROY TROPICAL MONORAIL
Grand Canal
THE VENETIAN
Madame Tussauds
HARRAH'S
THE MIRAGE (HARD ROCK INTERNATIONAL)
The Forum
THE LINQ
HARRAH'S/THE LINQ STATION
Las Vegas High Roller
LAS VEGAS MONORAIL
KOVAL LANE
WINNICK AVENUE
AUDRIE ST.
ALBERT AVENUE
N

The North Strip

Another one rises from the dust

Only in 2016 did it seem like another veteran fixture was vanishing from the Strip skyline without replacement; the Riviera's one surviving tower, a year on from the casino finally closing its doors after six decades, was felled in a controlled explosion. When built in 1955, by a consortium ranging from mobsters to the Marx Brothers, it was the Strip's first high-rise resort, designed to evoke French Mediterranean glamour. With nine storeys, it was also home to the Strip's first elevator.

During the first two decades of the 21st century, as neighbours like the Stardust, the Westward Ho, and Silver City were, one by one, blasted into oblivion, the Riviera's neon starburst facade had remained a welcome flash of colour on the North Strip. It was always a losing battle, though, and it's a sign of the times that it was ultimately purchased not by a casino operator, but by the Las Vegas Convention & Visitors Authority, which paid a reported $182.5 million to make room for a proposed expansion of the city's Convention Center.

However, casinos are returning to this patch. Resorts World Las Vegas (see page 75), a multibillion-dollar casino open on the old site of Stardust in 2021. Meanwhile Fontainebleau (see page 75) opened in late 2023 on the old site of El Rancho Hotel and Casino.

city's original patron, the other by a winged lion representing St Mark, who became its patron in 1204.

The interior of the Venetian holds fewer specific echoes of the city. While it's the **Grand Canal** upstairs that draws in the sightseers, it's the sheer opulence elsewhere, from the huge staircases and resplendent frescoes to the endless hallways of marble tiles, which makes this the most impressive public space on the Strip. It's also among the busiest, thanks to an excellent crop of restaurants, shops and theatres, and the Sands Convention Center at the back.

When it first opened, the Venetian out-trumped Bellagio's Gallery of Fine Art (see page 43) by opening two separate Guggenheim art museums. Both have long since disappeared, but the exhibition space near the hotel lobby is still used for occasional temporary art shows.

The Grand Canal

MAP P.64, POCKET MAP G4 & K5

The Venetian, 3355 Las Vegas Blvd S
Ⓦ venetian.com. Charge for gondola rides.
You can't have Venice without the **Grand Canal**. The Venetian has it twice – outdoors beside the Strip and inside, as the centrepiece of its shopping and dining mall upstairs. While neither section is particularly large, let alone authentic, you have to admire the sheer nerve. With its artificial sky, the indoor segment is obviously modelled on the Forum and features a large plaza based on St Mark's Square. Singing gondoliers take paying customers on short gondola rides along the canal.

Madame Tussauds

MAP P.64, POCKET MAP G4
Venetian, 3377 Las Vegas Blvd S
Ⓦ madametussauds.com. Charge.
Entered directly from the Strip, just off the Venetian's attractive covered Rialto Bridge, **Madame Tussauds** taps into Las Vegas's craving for close celebrity contact by allowing visitors to get personal with waxworks ranging from Brad Pitt and Daniel Craig to the

bizarre body-painted Blue Men (even though they're not actually recognizable as individuals).

With the single exception of the President in the White House, for whom there's an extra fee, you're free to take unlimited photos of, and with, all of your friendly, new-found waxy playmates.

The Palazzo

MAP P.64, POCKET MAP H3

3325 Las Vegas Blvd S Ⓦ palazzo.com.

Although the **Palazzo** resort is supposedly entirely separate from the Venetian next door, no one takes the distinction seriously (including Apollo Global Management when they bought it alongside the Venetian in 2021); broad internal walkways enable visitors to step from one property to the other and barely notice the transition. Counted as a single unit, this would be, with over seven thousand rooms, the largest hotel in the world.

Considered on its own, on the other hand, the Palazzo is among the least interesting casinos in Las Vegas. As well as its own very high-end shopping mall and a decent crop of restaurants, it's home to the *Lavo* nightclub/restaurant, but has nothing of any interest for casual

Madame Tussauds

sightseers. Even the giant butterflies added to jazz up its central waterfall feature look more like one of rival Steve Wynn's cast-off ideas than anything truly original.

Wynn Las Vegas

MAP P.64, POCKET MAP J2

3131 Las Vegas Blvd S Ⓦ wynnlasvegas.com.

Steve Wynn, the man who's credited with inventing the new Las Vegas by opening first the Mirage and then Bellagio, bounced back from losing control of the Mirage organization by building his own self-named resort, **Wynn Las Vegas**, in 2005. He swiftly complemented Wynn Las Vegas with Encore and ran both until stepping down in 2018 amid a number of #MeToo allegations, which were either settled out of court or dismissed at court.

When Wynn bought this prime slice of real estate it held the fabled *Desert Inn*, where Howard Hughes lived out his final years in paranoid seclusion. Steve Wynn doesn't do secondhand, though; he blew the whole place up and set to work building bigger and better than ever. The result, a majestic bronze crescent soaring skywards alongside the similar Encore, is breathtaking. Rendered almost blind by a degenerative eye disease, Wynn loved to fill his casinos with vibrant, dazzling swathes of colour – hence the plush red carpets that sweep through the interior, leading to a flower-packed **central garden** where the trees are bedecked with fairy lights and lanterns.

Because Steve Wynn wanted every Las Vegas visitor to come and admire Bellagio and the Mirage, he gave them all sorts of crowd-pleasing novelties. Wynn Las Vegas, being targeted exclusively at the luxury end of the market with its array of consistently high-end restaurants and nightspots, holds fewer specific attractions and is therefore not quite so much of a must-see. Its most unusual feature is the **Lake of Dreams (free)**, an expanse of water illuminated at night with changing projections and peopled by mysterious mannequins. Unlike the Mirage's volcano, it was deliberately designed to only be visible to visitors from inside the property.

Encore

MAP P.64, POCKET MAP J1
3121 Las Vegas Blvd S Ⓦ wynnlasvegas.com.
Encore stands in the same relation to Wynn Las Vegas as does the Palazzo to the Venetian. Erected three years after its elder brother, in 2008, and joined to it seamlessly via plush corridors, it's every bit as lavish – this is where Prince Harry was photographed naked in 2012 – but offers little sense of identity in its own right. In a deliberate piece of provocative one-upmanship, Steve Wynn built it 11ft taller than rival Sheldon Adelson's Palazzo, unveiled earlier the same year. Adelson, it's widely believed, responded by opening a large, downmarket Walgreens pharmacy at the Palazzo's Strip-level corner, thumbing his nose at the pretentious shops preferred by Wynn.

Like all Wynn's properties, Encore is ablaze with colour, like an episode of *Sesame Street* that's brought to you by the colour Red and the insects Butterfly and Dragonfly. Other than the general air of luxury, its main strategy to bring in visitors is via entertainment.

The indoor-outdoor, day-night **Encore Beach Club** (aka EBC at Night; see page 75) has been a huge hit, not least with visiting British royalty, while Steve Wynn pulled off a genuine coup by luring country superstar Garth Brooks out of retirement for a long-term deal. Brooks has since moved on. Elsewhere on the property, the golf course out back is a giant tropical oasis.

Guardian Angel Cathedral

MAP P.64, POCKET MAP K1
302 Cathedral Way Ⓦ gaclv.org.
Of all the Strip's eye-catching architectural wonders, perhaps the most unexpected stands just north of Encore – the Roman Catholic **Guardian Angel Cathedral**. It was built in 1963, on land donated by the former owner of both the Desert Inn and Stardust casinos, Moe Dalitz, a Jewish gangster from Detroit. Seeking to improve his public image, he paid modernist architect Paul Revere Williams to design this sloping tent-like structure. A stained-glass window to the right of the altar serves as a memorial to the Strip as it looked in the 1960s, depicting long-gone casinos like the Sands, the Stardust and the International.

Resorts World

MAP P.64, POCKET MAP J9
3000 Las Vegas Blvd S Ⓦ rwlasvegas.com.
As many of the established players in the Las Vegas casino-operating game are turning their attentions towards the East, and particularly to Macau, so the East is turning its attention to Vegas. Opened in 2021 by the Malaysia-headquartered Genting Group, Resorts World answers the question: what if Steve Wynn opened a hotel that pandered to Chinese gamblers? Similar to the thin, curved monolith of Wynn, Resorts World connects two such structures, looking like a floppy '7' from above, decked out in smart reflective glass with red fringe (an auspicious colour in China). These buildings hold three Hilton-brand hotels: The Hilton, Conrad and the extra-upscale Crockfords.

The sprawling site's **Zouk** nightclub (see page 75) follows the Wynn model of using entertainment to draw visitors away from the far busier Strip locales further south, while **Resorts World Theatre** (see page 75) looks to go toe to toe with the likes of Bakkt Theater (see page 75) et al. for hosting big name music and

The Adventuredome

comedy shows. Additionally are 5.5 acres of pools for guests, along with **The District** shopping centre (see page 75) and **Famous Foods Street Eats** (see page 75), which attempts to recreate a street food market common to Southeast Asia.

Circus Circus

MAP P.64, POCKET MAP K8
2880 Las Vegas Blvd S Ⓦ circuscircus.com.
Guarded by the giant figure of Lucky the Clown – if you suffer from coulrophobia, or fear of clowns, you won't like Lucky one bit – the candy-striped big top of **Circus Circus** has loomed beside the Strip for half a century. Circus Circus was battered and isolated by the recession, with owners MGM abandoning plans to revamp the space before selling to TI owner Phil Ruffin in 2019. Although former neighbours including the New Frontier and the Stardust disappeared, leaving Circus Circus cut off from the Strip in general, it seems to have weathered the storms of recession and Covid. Now, new neighbours Resorts World and Fontainebleau add to the draw for this neglected stretch, potentially saving one of the few remaining survivors of the early Strip.

Circus Circus has always been a strange, unsettling hybrid of circus and casino. It famously attracted the scorn of Hunter S. Thompson, who wrote in *Fear and Loathing in Las Vegas* that "Circus Circus is what the whole hep world would be doing on Saturday night if the Nazis had won the war". When it opened, in 1968, as Jay Sarno's attempt to repeat his success with Caesars Palace, it didn't include any hotel rooms and charged customers an entry fee. At first it was very much an adult playground, reflecting the sleazier side of carnival attractions. It took a few years to hit on the formula it still follows, of catering largely to families by offering **live circus acts** and other child-oriented attractions. It is also one of the last few casinos with actual slot machines that accept quarters. Coupled with its low room rates, the result has been that Circus Circus has become the tackiest of the major Strip casinos.

Circus Circus is so huge that it's the only Strip casino to have an internal **monorail system**, to take guests to their rooms. With its low ceilings and endless corridors, lined with fast-food outlets and novelty stores, it's quite a maze, and it can be hard to find the mezzanine area that's home to the **Midway**. The circular stage here plays host to a constant succession of free circus acts, from trapeze artists and jugglers to tightrope walkers and, yes, clowns. Old-fashioned sideshows offer kids the chance to kick-start a lifetime's gambling habit by winning stuffed toys. They'll also love Splash Zone, Vegas's newest water park, with its water playground and thrilling slides.

The Adventuredome

MAP P.64, POCKET MAP J8
Circus Circus, 2880 Las Vegas Blvd S
Ⓦ circuscircus.com. Charge.
Las Vegas's largest theme park, the **Adventuredome**, is housed in a giant pink enclosure at the back of Circus Circus, a long walk from the Strip. Entirely indoors and on a much smaller scale than, say,

Disney World or Universal Studios, it's aimed very much at children. Adults may well enjoy the twisting, looping **Canyon Blaster** and the even more ferocious, ultra-steep **El Loco**, but most of the space is given over to Angry Birds simulator rides and the like.

Fontainebleau

MAP P.64, POCKET MAP M8
2777 Las Vegas Blvd S
Ⓦ fontainebleaulasvegas.com.

Built but never quite completed, the Fontainebleau has had the kind of dramatic story arc that seems very apt for Vegas. The casino was originally scheduled to open in 2008 and was already topped out when the banks footing the bill pulled their funding in the wake of the recession. After a slew of bankruptcies and new owners, it was finally slated to open in 2022, until the Covid-19 pandemic made it perhaps Vegas' least lucky casino. In 2021, the casino was bought back by original owner. At the time of writing, it looked to be second time lucky for the Fontainebleau, with a schedule to open in December 2023.

Sahara

MAP P.64, POCKET MAP L2
2535 Las Vegas Blvd S
Ⓦ saharalasvegas.com.

The veteran Sahara, a Strip fixture since 1952, fell victim to the recession and closed its doors in 2011. It was stripped of its former *Arabian Nights* minarets and comedy camels and given a glossy new facade, to reopen in 2014 as **SLS Las Vegas**. But by this point, this stretch of the Strip ironically became a desert with very little footfall. The Meruelo Group snapped it up in 2018, restoring it to the **Sahara**.

Calling itself a "boutique resort" despite having three hotel towers and over 1600 rooms, Sahara is an entertainment-based property pitched a rung or two below the Strip's top tier. It's home to a music venue and nightclub, **The Sayers Club**, plus big-name restaurants including *Bazaar Meat* and the sleek **CASBAR Lounge** (see page 75).

The vast empty lot across the Strip from SLS belongs to MGM Resorts. It was sold to Phil Ruffin along with Circus Circus in 2019.

The Strat SkyPod

MAP P.64, POCKET MAP L2
2000 Las Vegas Blvd S Ⓦ thestrat.com.
Charge.

At 1149ft, the **Strat** makes a conveniently colossal landmark to denote the northern limit of the Strip, even if strictly speaking it's located in the city proper, a full mile north of Circus Circus. It took a feat of engineering to build the tallest structure west of the Mississippi in the shifting sands of Nevada; amazingly, its foundations are a mere 12ft deep. Served by Deuce buses, but not the city's Monorail system, the Strat offers little for sightseers aside from the **Strat SkyPod** itself. Two observation decks, one outdoors at the very summit and the other indoors on the floor below, offer fabulous views over the city and provice fascinating displays explaining everything you can see. Most visitors are up here for kicks, however, to dice with death on the array of **Thrill Rides** at the top.

The Strat Thrill Rides

MAP P.64, POCKET MAP L2
2000 Las Vegas Blvd S Ⓦ thestrat.com.
Charge.

The top of the Strat serves as the launching point for several terrifying **thrill rides**, for daredevils only. **X-Scream** is a sort of giant boat that tips upside down a thousand feet above the Strip; **Insanity** is a crane that spins riders out over the abyss; **Big Shot** is a glorified sofa that free falls a couple of hundred feet. Worst of all is the **SkyJump**, in which harnessed jumpers step off a platform to plummet 855ft.

Shops

Bonanza Gifts

MAP P.64, POCKET MAP L3
2400 Las Vegas Blvd S ⓦ instagram.com/worldslargestgiftshop.

The self-proclaimed "World's Largest Gift Shop", where Sahara Avenue meets the Strip, is *the* place to buy Las Vegas souvenirs. Trinkets celebrating the city, old and new, include countless variations on the iconic "Welcome to Fabulous Las Vegas" sign and memorabilia from individual casinos, such as packs of used playing cards.

The District

MAP P.64, POCKET MAP B11
Resorts World, 3000 Las Vegas Blvd S ⓦ rwlasvegas.com.

Proving that there's an unlimited appetite for shopping in Las Vegas, Resorts World put many of their stores facing the Strip on opening in 2021. Inside, The District's centrepiece is a giant orb known as The Digital Sphere, running adverts and messages to shoppers, as well as creative animations. Stores are largely designer fashion boutiques such as Judith Leiber and Hervé Léger.

Fashion Show

MAP P.64, POCKET MAP G2
3200 Las Vegas Blvd S ⓦ thefashionshow.com.

The only stand-alone shopping mall on the Strip, and for most Las Vegas visitors the only serious rival to in-casino malls such as the Forum, the Fashion Show spreads through two two-storey buildings across from Wynn Las Vegas. Despite the eye-catching circular sculpture that dangles over the pavement, it's in no sense an attraction, simply a functional shopping destination. Unlike its Strip rivals, it's large enough to hold department stores including Macy's, Sak's Fifth Avenue, Nordstrom and Dillard's, as well as an Apple Store and the usual clothing chains.

Grand Canal Shoppes

MAP P.64, POCKET MAP K5
Second Level, Venetian, 3377 Las Vegas Blvd S ⓦ thegrandcanalshoppes.com.

Arrayed along the waterfront upstairs in the Venetian, the Grand Canal Shoppes may surpass Caesars' Forum for sheer chutzpah, but as a shopping destination the mall is not a serious match. It does hold a handful of clothing chains, such as Hugo Boss, but consists largely of souvenir and impulse-purchase stores, with a big emphasis on showy jewellery. The best part is the ornate vaulted ceiling, designed in a Renaissance style with frescoes of flying angels between the gold trim.

Shoppes at the Palazzo

MAP P.64, POCKET MAP K5
Second Level, Palazzo, 3325 Las Vegas Blvd S ⓦ thegrandcanalshoppes.com.

More in keeping with the smart stores of Wynn Las Vegas next door than the gimmicky tone of the nearby Grand Canal, the Shoppes at the Palazzo are scattered around the resort's second floor. Few casual visitors pass this way, so the atmosphere tends to be hushed. Exclusive fashion boutiques include Jimmy Choo and Diane von Furstenberg, and there are also several expensive jewellery outlets.

Wynn and Encore Esplanades

MAP P.64, POCKET MAP H2 & J1
Wynn Las Vegas, 3131 Las Vegas Blvd S ⓦ wynnlasvegas.com.

There's a separate esplanade of shops in both Wynn Las Vegas and Encore, though they're all but identical in their high-end opulence. For ordinary mortals, fashion boutiques like Alexander McQueen, Givenchy and Chloé, and watch stores such as Jaeger-LeCoultre and IWC Schaffhausen, make great window shopping.

Buffets

The Buffet at Wynn

MAP P.64, POCKET MAP J2
Wynn Las Vegas, 3131 Las Vegas Blvd S
Ⓦ wynnlasvegas.com.

Buffets are always a high priority for Steve Wynn and at Wynn Las Vegas he's got one of the best buffets in town. In a plush room that oozes belle epoque excess, this is buffet food at its finest, with dishes from lamb osso buco and smoked duck salad to scallop ceviche and sushi rolls. While serious foodies will always prefer a real restaurant, if you've got a large appetite or are in a group with varying tastes, you won't be disappointed. $$$

Circus Buffet

MAP P.64, POCKET MAP K2
Circus Circus, 2880 Las Vegas Blvd S
Ⓦ circuscircus.com.

It may be found at the other end of the spectrum from a Michelin star, but Circus Circus certainly knows how to put the budget in buffet (at least by Vegas standards). The horseshoe-shaped self-service counter includes half a dozen pasta dishes, grilled shrimp, fried chicken, as Asian station with spring rolls and noodles, a build-your-own taco station, and a carvery. $

Restaurants

Bouchon

MAP P.64, POCKET MAP H4
Level 10, Venezia Tower, Venetian, 3355 Las Vegas Blvd S Ⓦ venetian.com.

Thomas Keller's scrupulous evocation of a French bistro, hidden away on the tenth floor of the Venetian's Venezia tower, may not have novelty value, but it's a lovely, relaxed spot, with plentiful outdoor seating and food that's nothing short of *magnifique*. Brunch is the best value, with sandwiches or quiche; dinner

The District

mains include French classics such as *steak frites* or *sole meunière*. $$$

Crossroads Kitchen

MAP P.64, POCKET MAP B11
Resorts World, 3000 Las Vegas Blvd S
ⓦ rwlasvegas.com.

Vegetarians and vegans tend to get marginalized by the hundreds of restaurants in Vegas, what with the penchant for steak and lobster here. But positive change is afoot, and Resorts World boasts Crossroads Kitchen, the Strip's first exclusively plant-based fine dining restaurant, which opened in 2022. The dishes are exquisite, with kelp caviar, stuffed zucchini blossoms and just a few of the sophisticated creations from head chef Tal Ronnen and his team. There's also an excellent tasting menu. $$

Delmonico

MAP P.64, POCKET MAP H3
Casino Level, Venetian, 3355 Las Vegas Blvd S ⓦ venetian.com.

Renowned for bringing New Orleans food to the nation, chef Emeril Lagasse has made the Venetian the setting for a sophisticated steakhouse with a strong contemporary flavour. While the lunch menu centres on salads and sandwiches, the big guns come out in the evening, with giant juicy steaks and starters such as red king crab legs or barbecue shrimp. $$$

estiatorio Milos

MAP P.64, POCKET MAP H4
Casino Level, Venetian, 3355 Las Vegas Blvd S ⓦ venetian.com.

Vast Greek amphorae adorn this beautiful restaurant, where the fish and fresh vegetables are on display in an airy dining space. For lunch there's a fantastic set menu, while in the evening your choice from the array of fresh fish, flown in daily from Athens, will arrive at your table cooked to perfection. $$

Grand Lux Cafe

MAP P.64, POCKET MAP H3
Casino Level, Palazzo, 3325 Las Vegas Blvd S ⓦ venetian.com.

Although it's owned by the Cheesecake Factory chain, and has itself gone national, the *Grand Lux Cafe* was originally created as a casual, but nonetheless classy, 24-hour coffee shop for the Venetian, and swiftly added this slightly smarter branch in the Palazzo. Both offer wide-ranging menus of fresh, well-prepared favourites from around the world at good prices – top options include pizza and salad, Salisbury steak, or Cajun shrimp and chicken jambalaya – and have their own on-site bakeries. $$

Lavo Italian Restaurant & Lounge

MAP P.64, POCKET MAP H3
Casino Level, Palazzo, 3325 Las Vegas Blvd S ⓦ lavolv.com.

Considering it's attached to the exclusive *Lavo* nightclub, this is an oddly traditional Italian restaurant, dark and romantic rather than loud or brash. The food, too, is rich and authentic, and the prices relatively restrained, with pizzas, pasta specials a little more and Mediterranean classics like veal *parmigiano*. $$$

Pantry

MAP P.64, POCKET MAP F4
Mirage, 3400 Las Vegas Blvd S
ⓦ mirage.com.

Located at the heart of the Mirage by the guest elevators. Serves wholesome lunch favourites such as soups, salads and loaded sandwiches, with breakfast available round-the-clock for your fix of fluffy pancakes, breakfast burritos, and eggs in various guises. $$

Pho

MAP P.64, POCKET MAP G3
TI, 3300 Las Vegas Blvd S
ⓦ treasureisland.com.

You could easily fail to notice that half the time, half of TT's 24-hour *Coffee Shop* is given over to this inexpensive Vietnamese diner. The pho of the name is steaming noodle soup; prices depend on the meat or fish, should you choose to add it. They also serve spring rolls, dry noodle dishes and sneak in some sushi options and Chinese favourites, too. $$

Red 8

MAP P.64, POCKET MAP J2
Wynn Las Vegas, 3131 Las Vegas Blvd S
Ⓦ wynnlasvegas.com.
This decadent, deep-red, pan-Asian restaurant makes a stylish retreat from Wynn's adjoining casino floor and serves a full menu of Chinese classics, from dim sum dumplings to chow mein or *ho fun* noodles, as well as Thai fish cakes and Malaysian satay and *laksa*. $$

Sinatra

MAP P.64, POCKET MAP J1
Encore, 3121 Las Vegas Blvd S
Ⓦ wynnlasvegas.com.
The Sinatra name, licensed by Frank's family, is of course a gimmick, but it tells you what to expect – the kind of idealized Italian restaurant the Rat Pack might have frequented back in the 1960s, formal and romantic and not in the slightest bit calorie-conscious. Ol' Blue Eyes is everywhere, from the speakers to the menu, with his favourite spaghetti and clams and osso buco "My Way" on the menu. $$$

Tao Asian Bistro

MAP P.64, POCKET MAP J5
Second Level, The Venetian, 3355 Las Vegas Blvd S Ⓦ venetian.com.
Tao is a place to come for the experience – the over-the-top opium-den decor, the giant Buddha statue, the crowds of dressed-up clubbers getting ready to party in the *Tao* **nightclub** next door – as much as the showy

Wazuzu

Asian food. And the food is good – pork or duck with sizzling fried rice, and steak or sea bass. $$

Top of the World

MAP P.64, POCKET MAP L2
2000 Las Vegas Blvd S
Ⓦ thestrat.com.
While it's a lot classier than the hotel-casino far below, this restaurant only stands out for the compelling reason that it's over 800ft up in the air and revolves every 80 minutes to give magnificent views over the Strip, Las Vegas and the desert beyond. Lunchtime (sandwiches and steaks) is the cheapest time, but dinner at sunset is much more romantic. $$$

Wazuzu

MAP P.64, POCKET MAP J1
Encore, 3121 Las Vegas Blvd S
Ⓦ wynnlasvegas.com.
Approached by an avenue of six colossal gilt pears, and featuring a huge crystal dragon squirming along its back wall, *Wazuzu* is by

far the best-looking restaurant in Encore, and it serves the best food too. As well as sushi, it draws on Asian cuisines such as Japan (seaweed salad), Mongolia (wok-tossed beef) and Thailand (chicken basil stir-fry). Be sure to try the *sake* too. $$

Yardbird Southern Table & Bar

MAP P.64, POCKET MAP K5
The Venetian, 3355 Las Vegas Blvd S
Ⓦ venetian.com.

Yardbird at the Venetian is the place to seek comfort in food, with classic Southern cooking, culture and hospitality. House specialties include chicken and waffles with a honey hot sauce, and lemon rotisserie chicken. Other big flavours with a distinctive southern lilt include shrimp n' grits and whole lobster mac n' cheese. $$$

Bars and lounges

Bar Parasol

MAP P.64, POCKET MAP J2
Wynn Las Vegas, 3131 Las Vegas Blvd S
Ⓦ wynnlasvegas.com.

A quintessential example of the Wynn way with design, these twin upstairs-downstairs bars, festooned with richly coloured umbrellas and filling Wynn's central stairway, are the perfect place to admire the Lake of Dreams. A cocktail or two, and you'll feel right at Las Vegas's absurd and exhilarating heart.

CASBAR Lounge

MAP P.64, POCKET MAP L4
Sahara, 2535 Las Vegas Blvd S
Ⓦ saharalasvegas.com.

Sleek interiors, including a sandy mirage-like ceiling feature above the bar, tan leather seating and mood lighting accompany this laid-back cocktail lounge. There's a daily happy hour from 3–5pm then again from 8–9pm and live

music every evening from the in-house DJs.

Gilley's Saloon

MAP P.64, POCKET MAP G3
TI, 3300 Las Vegas Blvd S
Ⓦ gilleyslasvegas.com. Charge to see live bands.

This lively country and rodeo saloon practically defines the new TI. Bikini-clad "Gilley Girls" ride the mechanical bulls, and you can join a free line-dancing lesson most nights at 7pm, drink two-for-one rum cocktails until 10pm, or dance to honky-tonk bands until long after midnight.

Peppermill Fireside Lounge

MAP P.64, POCKET MAP B11
2985 Las Vegas Blvd S
Ⓦ peppermilllasvegas.com.

A magnificent relic from the glory days, somehow surviving on the North Strip just north of Encore, this wonderful Vegas veteran outclasses any of the casino lounges with its pink neon, mirrored walls and central flame-spouting fire pit, and a spectacular assortment of colourful cocktails, culminating in its signature 64oz Scorpion. The attached diner serves an appropriately retro-flavoured food menu, from ham-and-egg breakfasts to pineapple-topped burgers and dinner steaks.

Señor Frog's

MAP P.64, POCKET MAP G3
TI, 3300 Las Vegas Blvd S
Ⓦ senorfrogs.com.

This totally raucous, hugely enjoyable indoor-outdoor Mexican-themed bar overlooks what used to be the pirate lagoon outside Treasure Island, and with its enormous open-air deck it makes a great spot for a sunset margarita or after-hours cocktail. As well as live bands on Fridays, they have a drag brunch every Saturday, followed by a Latin night with an open bar until 2am.

Señor Frog's

Clubs and music venues

Encore Beach Club

MAP P.64, POCKET MAP J1
Encore, 3121 Las Vegas Blvd S
Ⓦ encorebeachclub.com. Charge.

This luxurious multilevel complex of pools, patios, bars and private bungalows, in front of Encore but still thoroughly screened from the Strip, has to be the definitive expression of Las Vegas's recent craze for DJ-fuelled daytime poolside parties. No money could buy the worldwide publicity it received as the scene of Prince Harry Windsor's notorious antics in 2012, so not surprisingly it's now even more packed than ever. Exhausted revellers can escape the crowds either on pristine white "lily pads" out in the water or in private cabanas, but the pounding music will follow you everywhere. Expect to pay ultra-high prices even for regular bar drinks, let alone table service.

Tao

MAP P.64, POCKET MAP J5
Second Level, Venetian, 3355 Las Vegas Blvd S Ⓦ venetian.com. Charge.

An immediate hit in 2005 and still very much the place to be seen, this dynamic high-concept Asian-style nightclub inevitably attracts larger crowds than its small dance floor can handle. Even on the guest list you'll have to wait to get in and you'll pay heavily for any private space. The open-air *Tao Beach Dayclub,* by the pool, is a great place to gear up for the evening. Weekend wristbands also give admission to the same owners' *Lavo* club in the adjacent Palazzo.

XS

MAP P.64, POCKET MAP J1
Encore, 3121 Las Vegas Blvd S
Ⓦ xslasvegas.com. Charge.

Where do *Encore's* beautiful people go when they've had enough pool time at the beach club? To the even more decadent *XS* nightclub, of course. Stay in the tropical mood by throwing some moves on the massive dancefloor and drinking very classy cocktails.

Shows

Mystère

MAP P.64, POCKET MAP G3
TI, 3300 Las Vegas Blvd S
Ⓦ cirquedusoleil.com. Charge.

Twenty-five years since it first opened at Treasure Island, Las Vegas's original Cirque du Soleil show is still arguably the best – you can see why it changed the Strip's entertainment scene forever, overnight. *Mystère* is pure spectacle, from its gorgeous costumes and billows of cascading silk to jaw-dropping circus skills and phenomenal feats of strength.

Resorts World Theatre

MAP P.64, POCKET MAP B11
Resorts World, 3000 Las Vegas Blvd S
Ⓦ rwlasvegas.com. See website for schedule.

Attempting to muscle in on the long-term musician residency game of Caesars and Planet Hollywood, new kind on the block Resorts World has opened 4700-seat theatre, where major artists such as Katy Perry and Carrie Underwood have held significant multi-month runs over select dates. Comedians such as Kevin Hart also tour here.

The Venetian Theatre

MAP P.64, POCKET MAP H4
Venetian, 3355 Las Vegas Blvd S
Ⓦ venetian.com. See website for schedule.

The Venetian's largest of three events spaces holds 1815 people and hosts major music concerts from classic bands such as Earth, Wind & Fire, and The B-52s, plus international musical acts. The Atomic Saloon Show features raunchy Wild West-themed acrobatics. Big-name comedians occasionally drop in here as well.

Resorts World Theatre

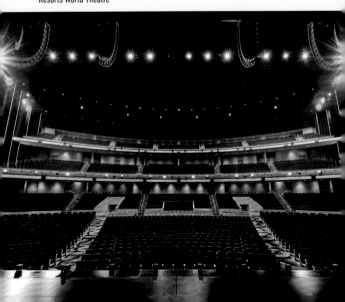

Little White Wedding Chapel

Wedding chapels

Chapel of the Bells

MAP P.64, POCKET MAP L3
2233 Las Vegas Blvd S
Ⓦ chapelofthebellslasvegas.com.
Crammed up against the singularly
unprepossessing *Fun City Motel*,
just north of Sahara Avenue, this
little chapel conceals a romantic
heart beneath its garish exterior.
Draped in white silk, with the
sun streaming in, it's really quite
attractive – and if it was good
enough for Pele, it's good enough
for you. Non-denominational
weddings are available; if you're
prepared to pay more, transport to
and from your hotel, plus a DVD
of the service are included.

Chapel of the Flowers

MAP P.64, POCKET MAP M1
1717 Las Vegas Blvd S Ⓦ littlechapel.com.
With three separate chapels opening
onto the same garden and couples
queuing to take snaps at the
waterfall, things can get a bit hectic
at peak times, but in principle it's all
surprisingly tasteful. Most popular
is the Victorian chapel, with its
marble floors and mahogany
pews. Packages are categorized as
Intimate, Elegant, Legendary, or
Specialty. Vow renewal packages are
also available.

Little White Wedding Chapel

MAP P.64, POCKET MAP F14
1301 Las Vegas Blvd S
Ⓦ alittlewhitechapel.com.
The definitive only-in-Vegas
wedding chapel, as used by Joan
Collins and Michael Jordan, not
to mention Britney, has grown
and grown to include five separate
chapels. Four resemble reasonably
pleasant areas in, say, a chain hotel;
the fifth, the notorious "Tunnel
of Love", is basically the former
driveway, roofed over with angels
painted on the ceiling, and hosts
drive-through weddings (BYOC -
bring your own car).

Downtown Las Vegas

Amounting, as far as visitors are concerned, to little more than three or four blocks, downtown is where Las Vegas started out when the railroad arrived in 1905, and also held its first casinos back in the 1930s. Many visitors prefer downtown to the Strip, feeling that by offering serious gambling, plus cheap bars, restaurants and buffets, its no-nonsense casinos represent the "real" Las Vegas. With its old-style neon signs and garish arrays of multicoloured light bulbs, it also looks much more like the Las Vegas of popular imagination than the high-tech Strip, while in the artificial sky of the Fremont Street Experience canopy it boasts a genuine must-see attraction. What's more, thanks to revitalization efforts that include the opening of the intriguing Mob Museum and the highbrow Smith Center, a classy performing arts theatre, downtown is back on top.

Fremont Street Experience

MAP P.80, POCKET MAP G12
Fremont St, between Main and Fourth sts
Ⓦ vegasexperience.com. Free.

Wanting to give downtown a large-scale spectacle to match the Strip and make visitors feel safer outdoors at night, the downtown casinos came up with an amazing rebranding scheme – they put a roof over four city blocks and renamed downtown the **Fremont Street Experience**. The sky itself seems to become a giant movie screen – a dazzling light show of monsters and mayhem. Live bands pump out rock classics on stages set up at the main intersections – and downtown parties until long after midnight.

SlotZilla

MAP P.80, POCKET MAP G12
Fremont St Ⓦ vegasexperience.com.
Weight restrictions apply. Charge.

Unveiled in 2013, **SlotZilla** is an extraordinary two-tier zip line centring on the world's biggest slot machine. The 120ft-tall monstrosity ejects four riders at a time on each

level. The lower Zipline has seats; riders on the upper Zoomline fly like Superman through the canopy of the Fremont Street Experience.

The Plaza

MAP P.80, POCKET MAP F11
1 N Main St Ⓦ plazahotelcasino.com.

Once Las Vegas's railroad station, the huge **Plaza** casino looked set to shut up shop in 2010. Surprisingly, it reopened within a year following a $35 million face-lift. Its owners cannily bought up the furnishings of the then-abandoned Fontainebleau, and the re-vamped Plaza now holds some of downtown's best bars and restaurants, including Oscar Goodman's glass-domed steakhouse (see page 83).

The Golden Gate

MAP P.80, POCKET MAP G11
1 E Fremont St Ⓦ goldengatecasino.com.

Having opened in 1906, the **Golden Gate** is only a year younger than the city itself. A railroad hotel before becoming a casino, it still has only a hundred rooms and remains an appealing historical anomaly. Recent modernizations have stripped away some of its charms, unfortunately.

Golden Nugget

MAP P.80, POCKET MAP G12
129 E Fremont St Ⓦ goldennugget.com/lasvegas.

Downtown's largest and highest-profile casino, the **Golden Nugget** has more in common with the Strip than with its neighbours. Built in 1946, it's among the city's oldest casinos, but its current incarnation owes more to the 1970s, when it was acquired by a young man who was to become the leading entrepreneur of modern Las Vegas: Steve Wynn. Downtown has traditionally been characterized by "sawdust joints"; Wynn gave the Golden Nugget the bright, glittery feel it retains to this day.

The most visible result of remodelling by its latest owners is the open-air swimming pool at its heart; guests who plummet down its towering waterslide pass in a clear tube through a shark-filled aquarium.

Most recently, the casino opened up its Fremont Street facade, adding *Bar 46* to create a prime vantage point for the light show on Fremont Street. The casino holds little for sightseers other than an actual golden nugget; the 62-pound, million-dollar Hand of Faith was found in Australia in 1980.

Binion's Gambling Hall

MAP P.80, POCKET MAP G12
128 E Fremont St Ⓦ binions.com.

If you think owning a casino is a sure-fire way to make money, **Binion's Gambling Hall** offers a salutary lesson. When its original owner, Benny Binion, died in 1989, this was, as Binion's Horseshoe, Las Vegas's most profitable casino. His heirs ran the place so badly that it lost its rooms and even its name. Caesars Entertainment briefly bought it to acquire the Horseshoe name and the World Series of Poker, but sold it on.

Binion's today is in a sorry state, with big empty spaces devoid even of slot machines. Its one gimmick is that visitors can pose for free photos with a million dollars in cash; it takes half an hour to get your print.

Fremont Street Experience

Four Queens

MAP P.80, POCKET MAP G12

202 E Fremont St ⓦ fourqueens.com.

Opened in 1966 and named for its owner's four daughters, the **Four Queens** fills a whole block of Fremont Street. Its basic role is to soak up any spillover from the Golden Nugget; it holds little apart from a decent pub, the *Chicago Brewing Company* and the *Canyon Club* showroom/nightclub.

Fremont Hotel

MAP P.80, POCKET MAP G12

200 E Fremont St ⓦ fremontcasino.com.

Ranking a distant second behind the Golden Nugget in terms of glitz and glamour, but still ahead of its other downtown neighbours, the **Fremont Hotel** is a smart but otherwise unremarkable casino. Back in 1956 this was Nevada's tallest building; now it's noteworthy as the home of above-par restaurants, and little else.

The D

MAP P.80, POCKET MAP G12

301 E Fremont St ⓦ thed.com.

A rare example of a casino completely changing both its image and its name, **The D** was until a decade ago a fake-Irish joint called Fitzgeralds, guarded by Mr O'Lucky the leprechaun. The "D" stands for downtown and Detroit, hometown of owner, Derek Stevens. He's taken advantage of the most unusual feature, that the casino has two storeys, to give each a different character – a contemporary style at street level, where go-go dancers gyrate in the "party pit", and vintage upstairs. Entertainment includes live music and comedy, plus a murder-mystery dinner theatre.

El Cortez

MAP P.80, POCKET MAP H12

600 E Fremont St

ⓦ elcortezhotelcasino.com.

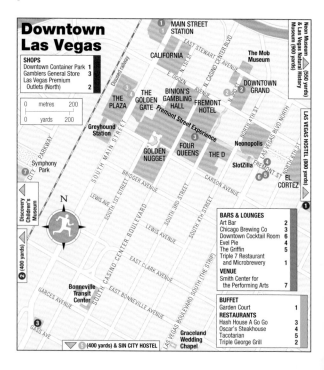

Downtown Las Vegas

SHOPS
Downtown Container Park 1
Gamblers General Store 3
Las Vegas Premium
Outlets (North) 2

BARS & LOUNGES
Art Bar 2
Chicago Brewing Co 3
Downtown Cocktail Room 6
Evel Pie 4
The Griffin 5
Triple 7 Restaurant
and Microbrewery 1
VENUE
Smith Center for
the Performing Arts 7

BUFFET
Garden Court 1
RESTAURANTS
Hash House A Go Go 3
Oscar's Steakhouse 4
Tacotarian 5
Triple George Grill 2

El Cortez

Long celebrated as downtown's most cheerfully downmarket casino, the eighty-year-old **El Cortez** is looking remarkably spruce thanks to a freshly remodelled façade and interior. For a taste of days gone by, as well as cheap dining and some of the best gambling odds around, it's worth braving the slightly intimidating five-minute walk east of the Fremont Street Experience even if you're not staying here.

Main Street Station

MAP P.80, POCKET MAP G11
200 N Main St Ⓦ mainstreetcasino.com.
At a little over twenty years old, **Main Street Station**, just north of the Plaza, is downtown's youngest major casino. Despite its antique-filled Victoriana theme, it's also among the brightest casinos. While it doesn't belong to the Station chain ubiquitous elsewhere in the city, it offers a similar range of restaurants and bars.

The Neon Museum

MAP P.80, POCKET MAP H10
770 Las Vegas Blvd N Ⓦ neonmuseum.org.
Charge.

If your appetite is whetted by the vintage signs displayed along Fremont Street, east of Las Vegas Boulevard, take a tour of the **Neon Museum** half a mile north. Treasuring signs and sculptures salvaged from long-lost casinos like the Desert Inn and the Hacienda, this is basically a junkyard, without even restrooms. Come after dark to see it at its best. The visitor centre was once the space-age lobby of *La Concha Motel*.

The Mob Museum

MAP P.80, POCKET MAP G11
300 Stewart Ave Ⓦ themobmuseum.org.
Charge.
Opened on February 14, 2012, the 83rd anniversary of the Saint Valentine's Day Massacre, Las Vegas's **Mob Museum** was designed as the lynchpin of a campaign by then-mayor Oscar Goodman – a former lawyer who defended many underworld figures – to revitalize downtown as a tourist destination. Its full name, the National Museum of Organized Crime and Law Enforcement, reflects its dual goal of chronicling the mobsters who once controlled the city

and the lawmen who eventually brought them down.

The museum takes up three storeys of the imposing former federal courthouse, two blocks north of Fremont Street. One upstairs courtroom has been restored to how it looked in 1950 when it hosted hearings by Senator Estes' Senate committee investigating organized crime.

With its comprehensive displays giving the inside stories on all sorts of Las Vegas characters and conspiracies, the Mob Museum is a fascinating place to spend a few hours. It likes to pitch itself as offering a serious perspective on the city's entanglement with the underworld; however, it has a disconcerting propensity for trivializing or glamorizing Las Vegas's gangster past. Lurid panels detail, for example, the "Mob's Greatest Hits", while waxworks depict gory corpses.

Discovery Children's Museum

MAP P.80, POCKET MAP F12
360 Promenade Place Ⓦ discoverykidslv. org. Charge.

Safely ensconced in spacious new premises, next to the Smith Center half a mile west of Fremont Street, the long-established **Discovery Children's Museum** remains a favourite with younger children in particular. Centring on the three-storey indoor Summit Tower, with twelve levels of interactive science exhibits, it also holds play areas such as a medieval castle.

Las Vegas Natural History Museum

MAP P.80, POCKET MAP H10
900 Las Vegas Blvd N Ⓦ lvnhm.org. Charge.
Collections at the **Las Vegas Natural History Museum**, a mile north of downtown, range from stuffed lions to animatronic dinosaurs, complemented by tanks of live sharks and snakes. One remarkable specimen, a dinosaur that was naturally mummified before it became a fossil, prompts an intriguing CSI-style investigation into its life and death. There's also a replica of Tutankhamun's tomb, donated by the Luxor when it stripped away its former Egyptian theme.

Las Vegas Natural History Museum

Shops

Downtown Container Park

MAP P.80, POCKET MAP H12

707 E Fremont St

Ⓦ downtowncontainerpark.com.

Located in the heart of downtown Las Vegas is this open-air shopping centre with unique restaurants and live entertainment. A 40-ft praying mantis with fireballs bursting occasionally from its antennae guards the entrance.

Gamblers General Store

MAP P.80, POCKET MAP F13

727 S Main St Ⓦ gamblersgeneralstore.com.

If you love gambling, but sometimes wish you got something back for your money, this is the place to come. You can buy anything from a pack of playing cards used at your favourite casino to a real roulette wheel, strategy books and non-gaming souvenirs.

Las Vegas Premium Outlets (North)

MAP P.80, POCKET MAP E13

875 S Grand Central Parkway

Ⓦ premiumoutlets.com.

A mile west of downtown and served by SDX buses (see page 117) from the Strip, this huge mall consists of over 150 stores accessed via outdoor walkways. Unlike the south-Strip branch (see page 32), most are genuinely "outlets" of well-known brands – Diesel, Tommy Hilfiger, Nike – so you can find real bargains.

Buffet

Garden Court

MAP P.80, POCKET MAP G11

Main Street Station, 200 N Main St

Ⓦ mainstreetcasino.com.

The only buffet to have bounced back in the Downtown area in the years following the Covid-19 pandemic is Main Street Station Casino's Garden Court, which is

Gamblers General Store

a relief to regular visitors as it is one of the few to offer quality at comparatively low prices. Stations include pasta and pizza, a meat carvery, southern cuisine, and depending on the time of day, cooked breakfast items. There's also a large dessert station and a small salad bar. $

Restaurants

Hash House A Go Go

MAP P.80, POCKET MAP F11

The Plaza, 1 N Main St

Ⓦ hashhouseagogo.com/vegas.

This gleaming, all-day diner is hardly the place for a romantic rendezvous, but its "twisted farm food" – obscenely large portions of wholesome American country classics like pot pie – tastes good and is great value. It's best for breakfast, with a varied menu and a few vegetarian options. $

Oscar's Steakhouse

MAP P.80, POCKET MAP F11

The Plaza, 1 N Main St Ⓦ oscarslv.com.

Perched in a glass bubble overlooking Fremont Street, this

shameless bid by former mayor Oscar Goodman to cash in on his larger-than-life image is a favourite with all who fondly remember the old Las Vegas. A New York-style steakhouse, serving quality filet mignon or bone-in steaks, it also has an Italian-heavy menu. The hostesses can be hired as dinner companions. $$$

Tacotarian

MAP P.80, POCKET MAP E14
1130 S Casino Center Blvd
ⓦ tacotarianlv.com.

This place is a jackpot for foodies. Taking the traditional taco and giving it a vegan spin was never going to win over the steak enthusiasts, but most meat eaters would be hard pressed to tell the difference. The tortillas are some of the best this side of the border, with barbacoa and chorizo soy alternatives soaked in lime juice and *pico* a perfect accompaniment to the homemade guacamole. $

Triple George Grill

MAP P.80, POCKET MAP G11
201 N Third St ⓦ triplegeorgegrill.com.

Oscar's Steakhouse

Its speakeasy decor, mixing brickwork with wood panelling, might not be genuine, but this downtown steakhouse is a real hangout for local politicos and lawyers. Come early for lunch and watch them wheeling and dealing in the back room over Caesar salads, airline chicken or steaks. $$

Bars and lounges

Art Bar

MAP P.80, POCKET MAP G11
206 N Third St ⓦ downtowngrand.com.

Just off the lobby of the Downtown Grand – formerly the Lady Luck – the *Art Bar* lives up to its name by festooning its ceiling with artworks. It is the ideal place to relax over a cocktail in its plush armchairs, perhaps after visiting the Mob Museum opposite.

Chicago Brewing Co

MAP P.80, POCKET MAP G12
Four Queens, 202 E Fremont St
ⓦ fourqueens.com.

Fremont Street's best bar and the pick of Las Vegas's few Downtown microbreweries is a noisy and upbeat spot to enjoy American, German and English-style beers, brewed on site and sold individually or in 64-oz "Growlers". They also serve pizzas, wings and sandwiches.

Downtown Cocktail Room

MAP P.80, POCKET MAP G12
111 Las Vegas Blvd S
ⓦ thedowntowncocktailroom.com.

Aimed at in-the-know locals rather than tourists, this small, dimly lit cocktail lounge, tucked away behind an industrial facade, evokes downtown's long-lost glory days. Expert mixologists create classic and original cocktails, plus there's an early evening bar menu and live DJs after 9pm (Tues–Sat).

Evel Pie

MAP P.80, POCKET MAP G12
508 E Fremont St Ⓦ evelpie.com.

Further along Fremont, just as the
casinos peter out, there's a clutch
of decent bars and restaurants. Evel
Pie, with its obsession with Evel
Knievel, rock music, pizza by the
slice, pinball machines and craft
beer wouldn't be out of place in
New York. Here, it's the coolest
place around to grab a slice and
a pint.

The Griffin

MAP P.80, POCKET MAP G12
511 Fremont St Ⓦ instagram.com/
lasvegasgriffin.

This cavernous downtown bar
is just a short walk from the
main cluster of casinos, beyond
the Fremont Street Experience,
but it's a world away from the
downtown norm. In-the-know
locals, including a strong hipster
contingent, weave through the
black velvet curtain guarding the
entrance to settle down by the
fireside or find a private booth.
Everything turns a bit more hectic
at weekends, when local bands or
DJs strut their stuff in the back
room.

Triple 7 Restaurant and Microbrewery

MAP P.80, POCKET MAP G11
Main Street Station, 200 N Main St
Ⓦ mainstreetcasino.com.

Join the lively, cheery drinkers
at this pub and restaurant, at the
heart of the antique-filled casino. It
serves award-winning microbrews
from Europe and elsewhere,
alongside substantial portions of
good pub grub. A roster of sports
on TV perfect the classic American
gastro-bar experience.

Venue

Smith Center for the Performing Arts

MAP P.80, POCKET MAP F12

Graceland Wedding Chapel

361 Symphony Park Ave Ⓦ thesmithcenter.
com. See website for schedule.

Las Vegas acquired a performing
arts centre in 2012 with the
opening of this showpiece Art
Deco-influenced theatre half
a mile west of downtown. Its
two-thousand-seat auditorium
hosts classical concerts, ballet
and touring Broadway shows,
while smaller showrooms put on
a varied programme of live music
and theatre.

Wedding chapel

Graceland Wedding Chapel

MAP P.80, POCKET MAP G13
619 S Las Vegas Blvd
Ⓦ gracelandchapel.com.

This pretty chapel, just south of
downtown, is "the home of the
original Elvis wedding". You can't
marry Elvis, and he's not a minister,
so he can't marry you, but he can
renew your vows. In the basic
package, the King walks you down
the aisle and sings two songs; for
triple the money you can get two
"duelling Elvises", young and old.

The rest of the city

A glance at any map will tell you that there's a lot more to Las Vegas than simply downtown and the Strip; well over two million people live in the valley as a whole. This is not a city where under-explored neighbourhoods harbour fascinating and little-known attractions, however. It's a vast and overwhelmingly residential sprawl that you'll need a car and plenty of time to explore at all thoroughly. Even then, almost all you'll find will be casinos, malls, bars and restaurants; this chapter highlights the pick of the bunch. In addition to the few that genuinely compete with the best of the Strip – the Virgin Hotels Las Vegas, the Palms and the Rio – it focuses on the so-called "locals casinos" throughout the city. While these can't match the wow factor of the Strip giants, they find their own niche by offering good-value food, drink and entertainment.

Area15

MAP P.88, POCKET MAP A11
3215 S Rancho Dr Ⓦ area15.com. Charge.
Area15 is huge art installation fronting a handful of quirky retail outlets, bars and entertainment facilities. At its heart is the highly interactive, high-concept **Omega Mart** from art collective Meow Wolf. **Dueling Axes** is an axe throwing parlour, and the **Illuminarium**, just to the west of the main building, is a high-tech planetarium. Combination or individual attraction tickets are available online.

Gold Coast

MAP P.88, POCKET MAP G15
4000 W Flamingo Rd Ⓦ goldcoastcasino.com.

M Resort

One of Las Vegas's first "locals casinos", targeted at city residents themselves, the **Gold Coast** was erected half a mile west of the Strip in 1986. While it swiftly acquired much fancier neighbours, in the shape of the Rio and the Palms, it's hung on to its rather staid Western decor, and remains geared towards a local crowd, especially from the city's Chinatown immediately to the north. As well as some good Asian restaurants, it also holds a seventy-lane bowling alley.

The Punk Rock Museum

MAP P.88, POCKET MAP B11
1422 Western Ave
Ⓦ thepunkrockmuseum.com. Charge.
Opened in 2023, this exploration of all things anti-establishment in the music world features artefacts and memorabilia from the early days through to the present. Highlights include the Jam Room where you can play instruments donated by various musicians, and items of iconic clothing, such as Debbie Harry's 'Vultures' shirt. Beyond the exhibition, you can grab a tattoo in the tattoo parlour, a drink at the bar, gifts and the punk shop and get hitched at the punk wedding chapel (presumably you're encouraged to pogo down the aisle).

Virgin Hotels Las Vegas

MAP P.88, POCKET MAP B16
4455 Paradise Rd Ⓦ hilton.com/en/hotels/
lasvgqq-virgin-hotels-las-vegas.
Richard Branson's first foray into the Las Vegas market was to buy the former **Hard Rock Hotel,** a mile east of the Strip, and reopen it as Virgin Hotels Las Vegas in 2021. Best seen as a self-sufficient party resort, it fills every weekend with southern Californians who come to soak up the atmosphere of its The Theatre, 4600-cap music venue and two-storey dayclub. The Casino, known as the Mohegan Casino at Virgin Hotels, is one of the few run by Indigenous Americans.

Area15

M Resort

MAP P.88
12300 Las Vegas Blvd S, Henderson
Ⓦ themresort.com.
Surveying the city from its hillside perch near the southern end of the Las Vegas Valley, ten miles south of Mandalay Bay, the shiny **M Resort** opened in 2009. Sadly, the economic climate was far from ideal for the smartest new off-Strip casino to be built in many years, so despite its impressive contemporary architecture and well-considered amenities it was soon struggling. Within two years, it was snapped up by Penn Gaming for barely a quarter of its original billion-dollar cost.

Through it all, the M is looking as good as ever – almost in the Wynn class. With lavish public spaces including a lovely Palm Springs-style pool complex and great restaurants like the hugely popular *Studio B* buffet and irresistible *Baby Cakes* bakery, it's unusual in appealing to locals and visitors alike.

Dig This!

MAP P.88
800 W Roban Ave Ⓦ digthisvegas.com.
Advance reservations essential. Charge.
Las Vegas has always specialized in making adult fantasies come true, but it took a truly inspired entrepreneur to come up with the

idea for **Dig This!**. On a patch of desert waste ground, ten miles south of Mandalay Bay, customers get to operate their very own piece of heavy machinery. On payment of a substantial fee, anyone aged 14 and over can drive either a bulldozer or an excavator for ninety minutes; that's a Big Dig, while a Mega Dig lets you do both. Not only do you not need a driving licence, you don't even need to be old enough to have one.

After a few minutes' training you're allowed to sit alone in your vehicle, linked via headphones to an instructor who has an override switch. In a bulldozer, you pile up a huge mound of sand and then power the dozer over the top; in an excavator, you dig trenches and play "basketball" using your scoop. The point, of course, is that it's all fantastic fun. Whether they do it as a retirement treat or a hen party escapade, everyone

who has a go seems to come away exhilarated.

National Atomic Testing Museum

MAP P.88, POCKET MAP B12
755 E Flamingo Rd Ⓦ atomicmuseum.
vegas. Charge.

Between 1951 and 1958, a remote desert area sixty miles northwest of Las Vegas, designated as the Nevada Test Site, was used for above-ground tests of atomic bombs. Mushroom clouds were visible from the city and tourists would time their holidays so they could watch the blasts. That astonishing saga is explored in the **National Atomic Testing Museum**, which covers not only the political, scientific and military background, but also the kitschy ways in which popular culture celebrated the bomb. A separate **Area 51** exhibit examines the even more unbelievable story of

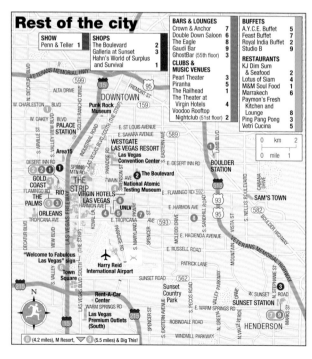

supposed "alien autopsies" in the same general vicinity.

Orleans

MAP P.88, POCKET MAP A12
4500 W Tropicana Ave
Ⓦ orleanscasino.com.

Owned by the same management as the Gold Coast (see page 86), to which it's linked by free shuttles, the **Orleans** is roughly a mile due west of New York–New York. Several of its restaurants and bars play on the New Orleans connection suggested by its name, but really the emphasis is on catering to more local tastes, via such means as an eighteen-screen cinema and 24-hour bowling alley. As a place to gamble at above-average odds and then relax over cheap food and entertainment, it's hard to beat.

The Palms

MAP P.88, POCKET MAP F16
4321 W Flamingo Rd Ⓦ palms.com.

It's a cruel drawback of running a relatively small off-Strip casino that as soon as you come up with brilliant ideas to lure visitors, the big boys simply copy your innovations and entice your customers back. When it opened across from the Rio in 2001, the **Palms** became the first Las Vegas casino to tap into the twenty-first century's mix of street and celebrity culture, with an array of youth-oriented clubs and theatres that made it the hippest hangout in the city. Since then, the Strip giants have added their own state-of-the-art nightclubs and the Palms has had to keep upping its game.

Despite recent money worries, the basic elements of the Palms' winning formula remain pretty much intact. In 2021, the Yuhaaviatam of San Manuel Nation assumed control of the casino, becoming Native American ownership of an entire Las Vegas resort. Nightlife options have since diminished as the focus was shifted towards gambling, although the

National Atomic Testing Museum

rooftop *GhostBar* cocktail lounge and the **Pearl Theater**, which ranks among the city's premier concert venues, are still major draws. The Palms even houses a world-class recording studio, used by artists from Lady Gaga and Katy Perry to Usher and Tony Bennett. And with its own cinema, some decent budget restaurants and a good-value buffet, it's careful not to neglect locals either.

Rio

MAP P.88, POCKET MAP H15
3700 W Flamingo Rd Ⓦ caesars.com/
rio-las-vegas.

A proud purple beacon, half a mile west of Caesars Palace across the interstate, when it opened in 1990, the **Rio** looked as though it might become the first casino in a generation to threaten the Strip's domination. It was independently owned and played on its Rio de Janeiro theme to build a reputation as the city's premier party scene for locals and visitors alike. Then, as now, all its guest rooms were sizeable suites, sold at highly competitive rates.

In 1999, however, the Rio was sold for almost a billion dollars to what later became Caesars Entertainment. Now run as an adjunct to its sister properties on the central Strip – to which it's linked by free shuttle buses (daily 10am–1am) from Harrah's (see page 55) and Bally's (see page 51) – it can therefore seem like something of an afterthought.

Every June and July, the Rio hosts the high-profile **World Series of Poker**; Caesars acquired the rights to the tournament when it purchased its previous home, Binion's Horseshoe, in 2004. For the rest of the year, it's best known for its sky-high *VooDoo Rooftop Nightclub* (see page 95), the Penn and Teller magic show (see page 95) and its fine selection of restaurants and buffets.

The Rio is also home to the **VooDoo Zipline**, a thrill ride that connects the rooftops of its two towers, nearly 500ft above ground level. Participants are strapped into exposed side-by-side seats, and the experience resembles riding in the scariest ski lift you ever saw.

Sam's Town

MAP P.88, POCKET MAP D12
5111 Boulder Hwy Ⓦ samstownlv.com.
Best known these days as the name of an album by Las Vegas's favourite home-grown band, The Killers, **Sam's Town** is a locals casino that stands six miles east of the Strip, alongside the main road out to the Hoover Dam. While maintaining its long-standing Wild West image, it has flirted in recent years with new affiliations such as NASCAR racing, hosting the now-defunct Sam's Town 300 race. It has also roofed over its central courtyard, adding gardens and waterfalls to create Mystic Falls Park, the scene of regular sound-and-light shows (daily 2pm, 6pm, 8pm & 10pm).

Sunset Station

MAP P.88, POCKET MAP D13
1301 W Sunset Rd, Henderson
Ⓦ sunsetstation.com.
The self-styled "Spanish Mediterranean" **Sunset Station**

casino was the first major casino to be built in the fast-growing suburb of Henderson, eight miles southeast of the Strip. It opened in 1997 as the flagship property of the so-called "Stations chain" of locals casinos, and while the chain as a whole has experienced financial uncertainties in recent years, Sunset Station itself is still looking good.

Its primary customers being drawn from its own neighbourhood, Sunset Station is crammed with community assets like the huge 72-lane, 24-hour StrikeZone bowling alley, a 13-screen cinema, and, rather more questionably, the Kids Quest daycare centre that'll look after children while their parents are gambling. Some of its features would be impressive even on the Strip, however, including the amazing undulating *Gaudí Bar* (see page 94), which is the centrepiece of the casino floor.

Westgate Las Vegas Resort

MAP P.88, POCKET MAP L5
3000 Paradise Rd Ⓦ westgateresorts.com.
The **Westgate Las Vegas Resort** used to be the largest and most famous hotel in the world. Built by legendary entrepreneur Kirk Kerkorian in 1969, half a mile east of the Strip, it was originally the International Hotel. Renamed the Las Vegas Hilton four years later, it earned its place in history by hosting Elvis Presley for 837 sell-out concerts, starting with his comeback appearance in July 1969 and continuing until his final Las Vegas appearance in December 1976. A bronze statue now commemorates the King's achievements. Neither having its own Monorail station nor standing next to the city's Convention Center spared it a battering by the recession, however, and in 2012 it went into foreclosure and lost the Hilton name. Its restaurants and music venues are still just about ticking along, but it feels rather peripheral.

Shops

The Boulevard

MAP P.88, POCKET MAP B12
3528 S Maryland Parkway
ⓦ boulevardmall.com.
A landmark for local shoppers since 1966 – long before anyone dreamed of opening stores on the Strip – the Boulevard mall is has suffered since closures of anchors Macy's and JCPenney. It's still a handy stop-off for day-to-day shopping.

Galleria at Sunset

MAP P.88, POCKET MAP D13
1300 W Sunset Rd, Henderson
ⓦ galleriaatsunset.com.
Massive suburban shopping mall across from Sunset Station, eight miles southeast of the Strip, with five department stores and a host of middle-American chains.

Hahn's World of Surplus and Survival

MAP P.88, POCKET MAP C10
2908 E Lake Mead Blvd ⓦ hahnsurvival.com.

True, no civilian really needs to acquire supplies and gear at an army surplus store, but this long-standing fixture of North Las Vegas is an experience to behold. It's packed with relics from the Vietnam War, bizarre books on hand-to-hand combat and other unlikely scenarios that may make for the weirdest souvenir of your trip.

Buffets

A.Y.C.E. Buffet

MAP P.88, POCKET MAP F16
The Palms, 4321 W Flamingo Rd
ⓦ palms.com.
A bright, modern space adjoining the main casino floor, the Palms' buffet (A.Y.C.E. stands for All You Can Eat) is popular with locals for its ease of access and range of world cuisines; be sure to sample the succulent ham hock. $

Feast Buffet

MAP P.88, POCKET MAP D13
Sunset Station, 1301 W Sunset Rd
ⓦ sunsetstation.com.

The Boulevard

Unlike their Strip rivals, all the Stations casinos still offer cut-price buffets to lure Las Vegans out to eat and gamble. Sunset Station has the nicest dining room; pick carefully and you can get a great-value meal including dishes like Indian curries, seldom seen elsewhere. $

Royal India Buffet

MAP P.88, POCKET MAP H15
Rio, 3700 W Flamingo Rd ⓦ caesars.com/rio-las-vegas.
Crowds flock to the Royal India Buffet to pile their plates with dishes from across North India; with all you can eat deals for both lunch and dinner. Freshly baked naan bread is served to the table. $$

Studio B

MAP P.88
M Resort, 12300 Las Vegas Blvd S ⓦ themresort.com.
Primarily this is a buffet, with food (and prices) to match the very best on the Strip, but it's also a "studio" because chefs demonstrate their art here on stage and TV screens. Prices include free wine and beer; the higher evening and weekend rates cover seafood spreads that include raw oysters. Allow time to get here – it's ten miles south of the Strip – and expect to queue to get in. $$

Restaurants

KJ Dim Sum & Seafood

MAP P.88, POCKET MAP H15
Rio, 3700 W Flamingo Rd ⓦ caesars.com/rio-las-vegas.
This offshoot of a popular restaurant in Las Vegas's nearby Chinatown has been an instant hit, especially for lunching locals who come to select dumplings and seafood specialities from the gleaming dim sum trolleys. Later on, full-sized mains like sizzling scallops or whole steamed fish are available. $$

Lotus of Siam

MAP P.88, POCKET MAP B12
620 E Flamingo Rd ⓦ lotusofsiamlv.com.
Lotus's reputation has followed it to its temporary home on Restaurant Row. The Northern Thai menu is famous for its garlic prawns and duck dishes, such as *khao soi*, strips of roast duck and crispy skin in a mild curry sauce. $$

M&M Soul Food

MAP P.88, POCKET MAP A11
3923 W Charleston Blvd ☏ 702 453 7685.
Genuine soul food being hard to come by in Las Vegas, this neighbourhood diner is a godsend. Four miles west of downtown, it's best reached by car; you won't be in a fit state to walk anywhere once you've filled up on a plate of their tasty fried chicken, ribs, gumbo or cornbread. $$

Marrakech

MAP P.88, POCKET MAP A13
6007 Dean Martin Dr ⓦ marrakechvegas.com.
All-you-can-eat banquets of rich, tasty Moroccan food, eaten with your fingers from low-lying tables where you sit on scattered cushions, is the style at Marrakech. Meaty couscous and pastry dishes are complemented by seafood alternatives, and followed by heavy desserts. Come to enjoy the Middle Eastern atmosphere, belly dancers and all; this is not a place for a quick meal on your own. $$$

Paymon's Fresh Kitchen and Lounge

MAP P.88
8955 S Eastern Ave ⓦ paymons.com.
A truly local restaurant, while not exclusively vegetarian – meat-eaters can enjoy dishes like the broiled chicken kabob and fish tacos – it's especially recommended for its extensive array of Middle Eastern classics such as falafel, hummus and *baba ghanoush*,

Ping Pang Pong

available singly or in a combination platter. $

Ping Pang Pong

MAP P.88, POCKET MAP F15
Gold Coast, 4000 W Flamingo Rd
Ⓦ goldcoastcasino.com.

You can tell straight away that this is the best Chinese restaurant in any Las Vegas casino; most of the diners are Chinese and the menu is written in Chinese characters as well as English. Dim sum makes a lunchtime treat, while later on you can get seafood noodles half a roast duck at good prices. $$

Vetri Cucina

MAP P.88, POCKET MAP F16
Floor 56, Palms, 4321 W Flamingo Rd
Ⓦ vetricucinalv.com.

North Italian cuisine is the metier of Vetri Cucina, where the views from the 56th floor of the Palms take in the skyline of the Strip. There's a traditional tasting menu,

or a la carte options such as roasted goat, grilled pork collar in a black pepper jus, and their giant 32oz prime dry-aged ribeye steak. $$$

Bars and lounges

Crown & Anchor

MAP P.88, POCKET MAP B12
1350 E Tropicana Ave
Ⓦ crownandanchorlv.com.

The closest Las Vegas comes to having a genuine British pub – complete with Cornish pasties, ploughman's lunches and Sunday roasts – although most of its customers, even when it's showing European soccer (or rather, football) games, are students from the nearby university.

Double Down Saloon

MAP P.88, POCKET MAP C17
4640 Paradise Rd
Ⓦ doubledownsaloon.com.

Double Down Saloon

Archetypal hole-in-the-wall dive bar, situated one block south of the Virgin Hotels Las Vegas. The interior features funky murals and a hard-edged punk jukebox. There are no-cover live bands most nights, plus slots, blackjack and pool, and signature drinks like "ass juice" and bacon martinis.

The Eagle

MAP P.88, POCKET MAP C12
3430 E Tropicana Ave ⓦ facebook.com/thelasvegaseagle.
This veteran of Las Vegas's gay scene, located four miles east of the Strip, has seen its glitzier rivals come and go, but the regulars still flock in for long-standing nights like the Tues & Fri underwear parties.

Gaudí Bar

MAP P.88, POCKET MAP D13
Sunset Station, 1301 W Sunset Rd, Henderson ⓦ sunsetstation.com.
The coolest bar in any Las Vegas casino, created in honour of Catalan architect Antoni Gaudí, this bizarre fungoid excrescence undulates through the heart of Sunset Station, with cracked-up mosaics across its cave-like walls and light courtesy of the colourful stained-glass panels in the ceiling.

GhostBar

MAP P.88, POCKET MAP F16
Floor 55, Palms, 4321 W Flamingo Rd ⓦ palms.com. Charge
From its 55th floor perch, the views of Vegas, particularly from the glass-bottom exterior patio, make for a pretty romantic setting. The Palms ownership have angled this very much at the top end of the market, both with the prices and their upscale attire only policy.

Clubs and music venues

Pearl Theater

MAP P.88, POCKET MAP F16
Palms, 4321 W Flamingo Rd Ⓦ palms.com.
See website for schedule.

The Palms' state-of-the-art theatre may be smaller than the Virgin Hotels Theater, but with its great sound and atmosphere it attracts its fair share of major-league acts across the spectrum, from hip-hop and R&B to reggae and rock.

Piranha

MAP P.88, POCKET MAP B17
4633 Paradise Rd Ⓦ piranhavegas.com.
Charge.

The jewel of the so-called "Fruit Loop" and the pulsating heart of Las Vegas's gay nightlife, the spectacular *Piranha* club is approached via either a fiery waterfall or a piranha-filled aquarium.

The Railhead

MAP P.88, POCKET MAP C11
Boulder Station, 4111 Boulder Hwy
Ⓦ stationcasinos.com. See website for schedule.

A run-of-the-mill member of the Stations chain of locals casinos, Boulder Station's one bright spot is this large lounge/theatre, which hosts Latin nights on Fridays and Sundays, but also puts on solid mid-range country, soul and blues acts.

The Theater at Virgin Hotels

MAP P.88, POCKET MAP B16
Virgin Hotels Las Vegas, 4455 Paradise Rd Ⓦ virginhotelslv.com. See website for schedule.

Virgin Hotels' flagship entertainment venue is this 4600-cap theatre, which attracts heaving crowds to see big-name touring acts, often from Latin America, such as Los Tucanes de Tijuana.

Voodoo Rooftop Nightclub

MAP P.88, POCKET MAP J15
Rio, 3700 W Flamingo Rd Ⓦ caesars.com/rio-las-vegas. Charge.

Long famed for its incredible 51st-floor views, this New Orleans-tinged rendezvous made its reputation as an ultra-hip drinking spot. Now a fully fledged nightclub, it's smaller than its newer rivals on the Strip, but the location is as good as ever and offers a great night out at more affordable prices.

Show

Penn & Teller

MAP P.88, POCKET MAP H15
Rio, 3700 W Flamingo Rd
Ⓦ pennandteller.com. Charge.

Magicians Penn (the talkative one) and Teller (the other one) have been performing at the Rio since 2000 – while still keeping up their TV careers – but the show remains fresh, whether you simply want to swoon at the magic or you love the behind-the-scenes tricks-of-the-trade patter. They're also great with their audiences, posing and signing happily for groups of fans after the show.

Gaudí Bar

The deserts

Las Vegas stands close to some of the most extraordinary landscapes on the planet – the stark, sublime deserts of the American Southwest. It's possible to get a taste of this red-rock wonderland on brief forays from the city, either to Red Rock Canyon, Hoover Dam and Lake Mead, or to the Valley of Fire. To appreciate its full splendour, however, you need to venture further afield. The primary goal for many visitors is the Grand Canyon, though you'd do better to visit the canyon's South Rim, almost three hundred miles east, than Grand Canyon West, which is closer to hand. Utah's Zion Canyon arguably makes an even better destination for an overnight trip from Las Vegas.

Red Rock Canyon

MAP P.98
17 miles west of the Strip
Ⓦ redrockcanyonlv.org. Charge.

For a quick blast of dramatic Southwestern scenery and searing desert sun, simply drive west on any road from the Strip. Tucked behind the first low scrubby hills, the **Red Rock Canyon National Conservation Area** centres on a desert basin at the foot of towering 3000ft cliffs. Ideally, come in the morning when the glowing red rocks are spotlit by the rising sun, and the day's heat has yet to set in fully. Staff at the visitor centre will introduce you to this unforgiving but beautiful wilderness, as well as point out the hiking trails and climbing routes that set off from the one-way, thirteen-mile **Scenic Drive** just beyond, which is the only way to see the canyon itself.

Hoover Dam

MAP P.98
30 miles southeast of the Strip Ⓦ usbr. gov/lc/hooverdam. Charge. Unscheduled maintenance issues mean full tours may not always be available but modified tours are usually offered.

The mighty **Hoover Dam** straddles the Colorado River and thus the Nevada–Arizona state line as well. While this graceful 726ft-tall concrete marvel does not, as many visitors imagine, supply a significant proportion of the electricity that keeps Las Vegas running, its construction during the 1930s triggered the growth spurt, and the gambling boom, that created the modern city.

The main highway to Arizona, US-83, crosses the Colorado on a new bridge, slightly downstream from the dam. To see the dam itself, leave the highway via the spur roads at either end. For a quick look you can park briefly on the Arizona side and walk out atop the dam. Otherwise, park in the multistorey garage on the Nevada side, and walk down to the Visitor Center. Displays there explain the story and inner workings of the dam, but paying just a little extra entitles you to join a Powerplant Tour, and ride an elevator down to its base. The hour-long Dam Tour takes you right into its bowels, to explore its dank and mysterious tunnels.

Lake Mead

MAP P.98
30 miles southeast of the Strip
Ⓦ nps.gov/lake/index.htm.

Created by the construction of the Hoover Dam, **Lake Mead**, east of Las Vegas, is the largest artificial lake in the USA when full. Its deep blue waters make an extraordinary contrast against the arid sands and red-rock cliffs of the desert, and attract huge numbers of visitors. Only its Nevada shoreline is accessible by road, most easily via Boulder City, a thirty-mile drive from the Strip.

Call in at the **Visitor Center** just off US-93, which has recently been expanded and renovated and holds some fascinating models and exhibits, then follow the **Lakeshore Scenic Drive** down to the lake itself. How close it approaches the shore depends on current water levels, which have remained low since 2002. Both **Lake Mead Marina** (Wriverlakes.com) and the neighbouring **Las Vegas Boat Harbor** (Wboatinglakemead.com) rent out boats and jet-skis, while the **Desert Princess** paddle steamer offers unique lake cruises (charge; Wlakemeadcruises.com).

Mount Charleston
MAP P.98

A real anomaly in the Nevada deserts, and one that tends to be appreciated more by locals than by visitors, the Spring Mountain range soars into the sky forty miles northwest of the Strip. Its highest peak, **Mount Charleston**, stands just under 12,000ft tall, so its forested slopes offer a welcome escape from the summer heat of the city. Several appealing hiking trails set off across the surrounding hillsides.

To reach the mountains, head northwest out of Las Vegas on US-95 then turn west onto Hwy-157, which snakes its way into **Kyle Canyon**. Up at the head of the canyon, the **Mary Jane Falls Trail** is a 2.5-mile round-trip trek that climbs via gruelling switchbacks to a pair of waterfalls. Half a mile further on, the three-mile **Cathedral Rock Trail** involves a demanding thousand-foot ascent to a promontory with onward views to Charleston Peak itself.

Red Rock Canyon

Grand Canyon West Skywalk

Lee Canyon along Hwy-158 to enjoy far-reaching views over the desert wasteland where Nevada's notorious A-bomb tests took place in the 1950s, and then return to US-95 via Hwy-56.

That's as far as most people go, but with a little more time you can drive north from Kyle Canyon to

Valley of Fire State Park

MAP P.98
Just over 50 miles northeast of the Strip, Ⓦ valley-of-fire.com. Charge.

The most mind-blowing red-rock scenery you can see on a driving day-trip lies in the Valley of Fire State Park. To get there, follow I-15 for thirty miles towards Utah, then turn right onto Hwy-169. The park begins just after you cross the ridge of **Muddy Mountain** to look out over a magnificent sandscape of incandescent, multicoloured peaks and cliffs stretching all the way to Lake Mead.

A roadside visitor centre explains local history and geology, and displays live rattlesnakes. It marks

The deserts

I.R.	Indian Reservation
N.C.A.	National Conservation Area
N.P.	National Park
N.R.A.	National Recreation Area
S.P.	State Park

NEVADA

Ash Springs

St George

Mesquite

Indian Springs

VALLEY OF FIRE S.P.

MOUNT
CHARLESTON
WILDERNESS

Mount Charleston ▲

Las Vegas

RED ROCK CANYON N.C.A.

Lake
Mead

LAKE MEAD
N.R.A.

Pearce Ferry

Guano Point
Skywalk

DEATH
VALLEY
N.P.

SPRING MOUNTAINS
N.R.A.

Hoover
Dam

Boulder
City

Temple
Bar

GRAND
CANYON
WEST

CALIFORNIA

Searchlight

Peach
Springs

Baker

Laughlin

Bullhead City

Kingman

Needles

| 0 | kilometres | 50 |
| 0 | miles | 25 |

the start of a five-mile, dead-end road that winds through amazing rock outcrops that can be explored on short hiking trails. The single most extraordinary formation, however, lies a further three miles along Hwy-169, where a natural arch – **Elephant Rock** – looks like a giant elephant poking its trunk into the sands.

Keep driving east, and you can loop back to Las Vegas along the north shore of **Lake Mead** – a total round trip of 130 miles.

Grand Canyon West

MAP P.98
125 miles east of Las Vegas Ⓦ grandcanyon west.com. If you drive here yourself you'll still have to join a ground tour. Charge.
The spot known as **Grand Canyon West** (or the West Rim) is not actually in Grand Canyon National Park, but on the Hualapai Indian Reservation to the west. Although it can be reached via a 125-mile one-way drive from Las Vegas, road

conditions are so poor that almost all visitors fly (see box page 101).

At this point, close to the western end of the Grand Canyon shortly before the Colorado River spills into Lake Mead, the chasm has dwindled to around two miles wide and lacks the extraordinary sculpted rock formations you may be expecting. Instead, Grand Canyon West consists of a cluster of viewpoints above drops of up to 4000ft, and looking across to similar cliffs on the far side of the river.

The major attraction is the **Skywalk**, a glass-floored, horseshoe-shaped walkway that juts out over the rim of a side canyon at Eagle Point, close to the airstrip where tours begin. The best view of the canyon itself comes from **Guano Point**, a mile or so north. The Hualapai tribe, who have lived here for over a thousand years, offer various other activities, including dance performances and barbecue cookouts.

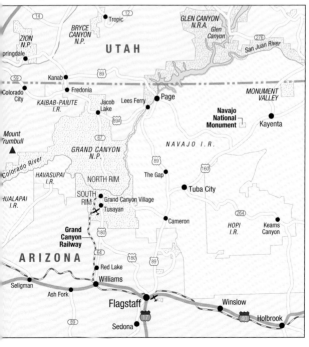

THE DESERTS

Grand Canyon South Rim

MAP P.98

270 miles east of Las Vegas Ⓦ nps.gov/
grca/index.htm. Charge. Tickets valid for
seven days.

To see the Grand Canyon in all
its glory, you have to visit **Grand
Canyon National Park**. This is the
area familiar from a million movies
and photographs, where the canyon
is studded with mighty red-rock
buttes and pyramids, and measures
a mile deep and eleven miles wide.

Tourist facilities, concentrated
around several magnificent
viewpoints along the canyon's South
Rim, can be reached either by road
– a total drive from Las Vegas of
270 miles, via the I-40 interstate
that crosses northern Arizona fifty
miles south of the canyon – or by
air, to Tusayan airport, six miles
south of the canyon.

While it's possible to visit
the **South Rim** on a day-trip (see
box opposite), it makes much

more sense to drive yourself and
stay at least one night. That will
give you the chance to spend some
time beside the canyon at sunset
and dawn, and to sample the
evening atmosphere of the splendid
old rim-edge *El Tovar* **Hotel** (see
page 112).

Zion National Park

MAP P.98

160 miles northeast of Las Vegas
Ⓦ nps.gov/zion/index.htm. Charge. Tickets
valid for seven days.

Any Las Vegas visitor hoping to see
the stupendous desert scenery of
the Southwest at its absolute best
would do well to consider making
a side trip to **Zion National Park**.
Located in southwest Utah, a fast,
direct drive of 160 miles northeast
up I-15 from Las Vegas, it's every
bit as impressive as the Grand
Canyon, and offers much greater
potential for an active weekend
excursion from the city.

Grand Canyon South Rim

Grand Canyon tours

The Grand Canyon is not as near Las Vegas as you might imagine. **Grand Canyon National Park** is two hundred miles east of Las Vegas, and the **South Rim** (see page 100), which holds the park's main tourist facilities and viewpoints, is a drive of almost three hundred miles each way from the city. To see the canyon on a day-trip involves a long bus ride and an expensive flight. The majority of tours from Las Vegas therefore go to **Grand Canyon West** (see page 99), more like one hundred miles from the city, which while less spectacular is also home to the **Skywalk**, and offers the chance to land by, and even take a rafting trip on, the **Colorado River**.

With most of the operators listed below, you can choose between taking a **tour** to Grand Canyon West or the South Rim, by bus, helicopter or plane. Bus tours to Grand Canyon West typically include the Skywalk as an optional extra. The entire round-trip takes at least twelve hours, including four hours at Grand Canyon West itself. A **bus tour** to the South Rim takes over sixteen hours, with less time at the canyon itself. Prices are higher for a deluxe coach.

Flight-seeing tours to Grand Canyon West are cheapest if by plane (without landing). Expect to pay more to experience the same route by helicopter. Prices are around 50 percent higher for a tour that includes walking on the Skywalk. If you're prepared to splurge on the experience, there's also a helicopter tour that lands down by the river in the cradle of the canyon as well.

All **flights** to the South Rim are in fixed-wing planes. Combo tours of a flight with a ground tour of canyon viewpoints by bus is also available, as are tours that include a flight to the area of the South Rim from Las Vegas and a separate helicopter flight over the Grand Canyon.

Note that many flights depart not from Las Vegas itself, but from **Boulder City**, thirty miles southeast. If you're hoping for an aerial view of Sin City into the bargain, check which airport your operator uses. Shop around as special discount prices are often available.

Tour operators

Grand Canyon Scenic Airlines ⓦ grandcanyonairlines.com.
Grand Canyon Destinations ⓦ grandcanyondestinations.com.
Grand Canyon Tour Company ⓦ grandcanyontourcompany.com.
Maverick ⓦ maverickhelicopter.com.
Papillon ⓦ papillon.com.
Sundance ⓦ sundancehelicopters.com.

Named by nineteenth-century Mormon settlers, and carved by the Virgin River, Zion Canyon stands at the heart of the park. Unlike at the Grand Canyon, which is almost always seen from above, visitors enter by following the river upstream from the south and therefore see it from the verdant valley below. Astonishing sheer red-rock walls soar to either side, many of them topped by crests of paler sandstone that have been given fanciful names like the Court of the Patriarchs and the Great White Throne.

At the northern end of the canyon, visitors can follow the easy, mile-long **Riverside Walk** to the point where the Virgin River enters the valley. In the Zion Narrows beyond, accessible only to hardy hikers happy to wade waist-deep in ice-cold water, the towering canyon walls stand just a few feet apart. Other demanding trails switchback out of the valley to reach the desert uplands high above, and make wonderful day-hikes; the **West Rim Trail**, for example, climbs to a slender rock spur known as Angel's Landing, with a sheer quarter-of-a-mile drop

to either side. Not surprisingly, Zion is also a favourite destination with rock climbers; several local operators offer guides.

Although it's possible to drive through the southern portion of the park, and continue east (towards Bryce Canyon) via an amazing 1930s tunnel, the only vehicles allowed into the narrowest part of the canyon are free shuttle buses, which depart from the visitor centre beside the park entrance.

In the canyon itself, the veteran *Zion Lodge* (see page 113) offers accommodation and dining, and the park runs large but very pleasant campgrounds. Otherwise, almost all facilities are in the gateway town of **Springdale**, in a magnificent setting just south of the park.

Zion National Park

Restaurants

Arizona Steakhouse

Bright Angel Lodge, Grand Canyon South Rim Ⓦ grandcanyonlodges.com. Nov & Dec closed.

This good-value restaurant, near the rim but with no views, is the most convenient place to pick up a decent meal on the South Rim. Lunchtime burgers, sandwiches and salads cinclude a few plant-based options. Dinners include options such as bison ribeye steak and green chile corn tamales. $$

Bit & Spur Restaurant

1212 Zion Park Blvd, Springdale UT Ⓦ bitandspur.com.

With a cozy saloon-like interior, and a terrace facing Zion's red-rock cliffs, this relaxed but high-quality Mexican/Southwestern restaurant makes a wonderful dinner spot. Excellent vegan and vegetarian dishes include sweet potato tamales. Elsewhere on the menu, smoked baby back ribs and *chile relleno* (stuffed chilli) are highlights, while the outdoor seating makes an ideal venue for a beer after a long day's hiking. $$

Canyon Restaurant & Bar

The Retreat on Charleston Peak, 2755 Kyle Canyon Rd Ⓦ retreatoncharleston peak.com.

With an emphasis on sustainability and buying local, much of the produce is sourced from farms nearby, from the proper coffee to crispy bacon. The European-inspired menu includes scallops and chorizo, pork loin skewer, and a daily special, served at round tables in a vaulted room. $$

El Tovar Dining Room

El Tovar, Grand Canyon South Rim Ⓦ grandcanyonlodges.com.

The stately splendours of the timber and stone-built *El Tovar* make an impressive setting for great food. Only the front row of tables enjoy partial views of the canyon, but this grand century-old hotel oozes old-fashioned charm and the waiters are happy to let you linger. Reserve ahead for dinner. Mains include half a duck and veal *wienerschnitzel*; lunch and breakfast are first-come first-served and much cheaper. $$

Mount Charleston Lodge

5375 Kyle Canyon Rd Ⓦ mtcharlestonlodge.com.

This is the obvious place to stop for lunch on a Mount Charleston day trip, where the road up the mountain reaches its dead end, featuring an outdoor patio that enjoys drop-dead views. The food itself includes brick over pizzas, mountain chili, and half-pound burgers. $$

Spotted Dog

Flanigan's Inn, 428 Zion Park Blvd, Springdale UT Ⓦ flanigans.com.

This very reasonably priced restaurant is attached to a motel near the Zion park entrance. In the morning it lays out a decent breakfast buffet, while the dinner menu ranges from a highly recommended lamb shank to meatloaf or pasta. $$

El Tovar Dining Room

ACCOMMODATION

Mandalay Bay Resort

Accommodation

Choosing where to stay is the single biggest decision of any Las Vegas trip. Las Vegas is not like other destinations, where it's the city that you've come to see, and your choice of hotel makes little difference. In Las Vegas, it's the hotels that you've come to see – or rather the stupendously large casino resorts that hold not only the hotels, but also the restaurants, clubs, theatres and attractions, as well as the slot machines and gaming tables. The fundamental choice is whether or not to stay on the Strip, which means staying in one of the colossal mega-casinos. Las Vegas is currently home to 32 of the world's 200 largest hotels, most along or very close to the Strip. Between them, they house over 80,000 rooms, an average of almost 4000 each. All of those rooms are at least the standard of a good chain motel. Many are much more opulent; the standard rooms at places like Wynn, the Venetian and Bellagio are very plush, while every property offers suites. However, the experience of staying in a hotel that has several thousand rooms has its drawbacks, including long check-in queues (half an hour is normal), a lack of personal service and endless walking to and fro. In, say, Caesars Palace or the MGM Grand, it can take twenty minutes to walk from your room out onto the Strip. The result is that most visitors spend their time in either their own hotel or its immediate neighbours. The alternative is to stay downtown, where every hotel is easy walking distance from the rest. But while downtown has more affordable gambling and dining, it has few shops, shows or clubs, and lacks the jaw-dropping architecture of the Strip. It's possible to find a room elsewhere in the city, in a so-called locals casino, or in one of the many chain motels, but it's not recommended for visitors who want to experience all that makes Las Vegas unique. As for rates, rooms change in price every night according to demand. If there's a hotel you'd really like to stay at, it's best to book a couple of months or more in advance. For weekday stays, you can get a real bargain at the last minute, but you will have fewer options. And when a mega conference or event is in town, all bets are off, because prices mushroom. The denominations given here are broad guidelines to suggest what you might pay during an ordinary, quiet weekday, not including resort fees (see box).

Resort fees and taxes

Note that in addition to the room rates shown in this chapter, guests in almost every Las Vegas hotel are also required to pay so-called resort fees. These additional daily fees were introduced on the pretext of covering internet access – even if you don't use it – and generally also include such things as local or even long-distance (at Wynn and Encore) phone calls, use of a fitness centre and a newspaper, but *not* parking.

Hotel rates shown here do not include the additional room tax added to all bills, of twelve percent on the Strip, and thirteen percent downtown.

The Strip

ARIA MAP P.40, POCKET MAP B1. 3730 Las Vegas Blvd S ⓦ aria.com. CityCenter's focal resort, Aria, is perfect for modernists. There's a sleek contemporary aesthetic, and the classy rooms feature big beds, walk-in showers as well as tubs, and on-screen digital controls for everything from curtains to a/c. Check-in can be slow and somewhat anarchic. **$$$**

BELLAGIO MAP P.40, POCKET MAP F7. 3600 Las Vegas Blvd S ⓦ bellagio.com. As Las Vegas is forever outdoing itself, Bellagio is no longer the cream of the crop, but by any normal standards its opulent rooms epitomize luxury, while its location and amenities can't be beaten. The premium rooms overlook the lake and its fountains, but the views from the back, over the pool, are great too. **$$$$**

CAESARS PALACE MAP P.50, POCKET MAP F6. 3570 Las Vegas Blvd S ⓦ caesars. com/caesars-palace. Fond memories of 1960s excess will always form part of the appeal of Caesars Palace, even if these days comfort tends to win over kitsch. The sheer scale of the place can be overwhelming, but with its top-class dining and shopping, plus a fabulous pool and spa, it still has a real cachet. For serious luxury, pay extra to stay in the newer Augustus and Octavius towers, with separate entrances for greater privacy. **$$$$**

CIRCUS CIRCUS MAP P.64, POCKET MAP K8. 2880 Las Vegas Blvd S ⓦ circuscircus. com. Long a favourite with families and budget travellers, Circus Circus is showing

its age; feeling a little like the casino time forgot. If you don't plan to linger and you have a car, its rock-bottom rates may prove irresistible. Pay a little extra to stay in its renovated towers, as opposed to the dingy Manor section. **$**

THE COSMOPOLITAN MAP P.40, POCKET MAP F9. 3708 Las Vegas Blvd S ⓦ cosmopolitanlasvegas.com. Stylish and contemporary, *The Cosmopolitan* is a great option at the heart of the Strip. The comfortable rooms come with colossal beds; even those that aren't suites have large living areas, while all except the cheapest have Strip-view balconies (a rarity in Las Vegas), and many overlook the Bellagio fountains. There's a spa plus top-quality restaurants and clubs, and the rooms aren't far from the lobby or the garage. **$$$$**

THE CROMWELL MAP P.50, POCKET MAP G7. 3595 Las Vegas Blvd S ⓦ caesars.com/ cromwell. Only in Las Vegas does having 188 rooms make you a "boutique hotel"; the Strip's smallest casino is known as an exclusive and expensive hideaway. Nightlife and free live entertainment are on-site. **$$$**

ENCORE MAP P.64, POCKET MAP J1. 3131 Las Vegas Blvd S ⓦ wynnlasvegas. com. Las Vegas doesn't come any more luxurious than this; Encore truly is fit for a prince (just ask Harry Windsor). The huge, high-tech rooms are more subdued and earth-toned than the lurid reds the casino might lead you to expect, and all are suites, although the beds are screened off from the living areas rather than being separate rooms. **$$$$**

EXCALIBUR MAP P.26, POCKET MAP B4. 3850 Las Vegas Blvd S Ⓦ excalibur.com. Cross the drawbridge, enter the Disneyesque castle, wheel your bag through the casino full of kids, ride the elevator to the top of the tower and amazingly enough, so long as you pay a little extra for one of the Royal Tower rooms, you've found yourself a nice place to stay. The older rooms are looking tired, though, and with its endless queues Excalibur itself can feel too big for comfort. **$**

FLAMINGO LAS VEGAS MAP P.50, POCKET MAP G6. 3555 Las Vegas Blvd S Ⓦ caesars.com/flamingo-las-vegas. So long as you stay at ground level, the *Flamingo* seems like a great hotel – light, airy and central, but on a manageable scale. It has an attractive garden complete with live flamingoes and a 15-acre Caribbean-style pool. The rooms upstairs are very hit and miss, though, and can be grubby. Therefore, only consider staying here if you find a truly exceptional rate. **$$**

HARRAH'S MAP P.50, POCKET MAP G5. 3475 Las Vegas Blvd S Ⓦ caesars.com/harrahs-las-vegas. There's nothing to quicken the heart about Harrah's, the middle-of-the-Strip, middle-of-the-road casino that spent a couple of decades catering so assiduously to its long-standing customers that it was able to buy all its fancier neighbours. With that kind of success, they haven't felt compelled to change much. Standard rooms are rather ordinary, though there are some swish suites. **$$$**

HORSESHOE MAP P.50, POCKET MAP G7. 3645 Las Vegas Blvd S Ⓦ guestreservations.com/bally-s-las-vegas. Staying at Horseshoe (formerly Bally's) is not an experience anyone gets very excited about – the rooms are spacious but otherwise run of the mill – but it is in a great location to make the most of the Strip. Above all, it's connected to its younger sister Paris, so guests get the benefits of staying there at much lower rates. **$$$**

THE LINQ MAP P.50, POCKET MAP G5. 3535 Las Vegas Blvd S Ⓦ caesars.com/linq. The former Imperial Palace always ranked among the Strip's cheapest options; now renamed The Linq, it's maintaining that tradition by charging surprisingly low rates for such a central location. **$$$$**

LUXOR MAP P.26, POCKET MAP B6. 3900 Las Vegas Blvd S Ⓦ luxor.com. More than twenty years since this futuristic black-

Las Vegas's most luxurious spas

State-of-the-art spas in Las Vegas's top casinos pamper visitors with pools, steam rooms, fitness facilities and massage services. Daily entry normally costs around $50, and massages and other treatments from around $100 per half hour. Often, during busy periods, only guests staying in the relevant casino can use its spa. The following are the very best:

Aria. The Spa. Ⓦ aria.mgmresorts.com
Bellagio. Spa Bellagio. Ⓦ 7bellagio.mgmresorts.com
Caesars Palace. Qua. Ⓦ caesars.com
The Cosmopolitan. Sahra. Ⓦ cosmopolitanlasvegas.com
Encore. The Spa at Encore. Ⓦ wynnlasvegas.com
Golden Nugget. Spa. Ⓦ goldennugget.com
Virgin Hotels Las Vegas. The Spa. Ⓦ hilton.com
Mandalay Bay. Spa Mandalay. Ⓦ mandalaybay.mgmresorts.com
Resorts World. Awana. Ⓦ rwlasvegas.com
Planet Hollywood. Mandara. Ⓦ mandaraspa.com
The Venetian. Canyon Ranch. Ⓦ canyonranch.com
Wynn. Spa. Ⓦ wynnlasvegas.com

glass pyramid opened, it's sadly feeling its age. It can still be a thrill to stay in one of the original rooms, with their sloping windows, but there's a reason rooms in the newer tower next door cost a little more – they're in much better condition, and also have baths instead of just showers. **$**

MANDALAY BAY MAP P.26, POCKET MAP B7. 3950 Las Vegas Blvd S Ⓦ mandalaybay. com. This far south of the central Strip, it makes sense to see Mandalay Bay as a self-contained resort. If you're happy to spend long days by its extravagant pool, and while away your evenings in its fine restaurants, bars, clubs and theatres, then it's well worth considering. The rooms are very comfortable, with both baths and walk-in showers. **$$$**

MGM GRAND MAP P.26, POCKET MAP C3. 3799 Las Vegas Blvd S Ⓦ mgmgrand.com. While it may not be the world's largest hotel any more, the MGM Grand feels too big for its own good; once you've queued to check in and walked half a mile to your room, you may not feel up to venturing out to explore. Accommodation has been largely upgraded at the expense of its former character; the dark brown palette could be any convention hotel, anywhere. **$$$**

NEW YORK–NEW YORK MAP P.26, POCKET MAP C3. 3790 Las Vegas Blvd S Ⓦ newyorknewyork.com. Spending a night or two in Las Vegas's own Big Apple makes a more appealing prospect than a stay at most of its larger, less compact neighbours. Whether you opt for a "Park Avenue" or a slightly larger "Madison Avenue" room, the guest rooms are attractive and readily accessible, with some nice Art Deco touches, and the casino itself holds some excellent bars and restaurants. **$$**

THE PALAZZO MAP P.64, POCKET MAP H3. 3325 Las Vegas Blvd S Ⓦ palazzo.com. Staying at The Palazzo is fundamentally the same as staying at The Venetian (once you go downstairs, you're in the same building), but you'll find yourself slightly further from the heart of the action here. The actual rooms are very similar, with plush sleeping and living areas at slightly different levels, and huge marble bathrooms. **$$$$**

PARIS MAP P.50, POCKET MAP G8. 3655 Las Vegas Blvd S Ⓦ caesars.com/ paris-las-vegas. For many visitors, Paris represents an ideal compromise – you get to stay in an interesting big-name property, with excellent amenities plus "only in Vegas" features like the Eiffel Tower outside your window – without paying premium prices for opulent fittings you don't really need. The standard rooms are slightly faded now; for a little more pampering, opt for a newer "Red Room". **$$$**

PARK MGM MAP P.26, POCKET MAP C2. 3770 Las Vegas Blvd S Ⓦ parkmgm.com. The long-standing but largely anonymous Monte Carlo underwent a major overhaul, and was split into two separate hotels – the 2700-room Park MGM and the pricier boutique NoMad (Ⓦ nomadlasvegas.com). Expect fancier rooms in brand new NoMad, more in keeping with the upscale CityCenter vibe. However, Park MGM rooms can be great value. **$$$$**

PLANET HOLLYWOOD MAP P.50, POCKET MAP G9. 3667 Las Vegas Blvd S Ⓦ caesars. com/planet-hollywood. While Planet Hollywood's confusing layout can make it a long trek from your car to your room, once you're here it's a great-value central location. The rooms are in a style they call "Hollywood Hip", which tends to mean black and gold carpets and wallpaper; movie stills on the wall; and walk-in showers as well as baths. **$$**

RESORTS WORLD MAP P.64, POCKET MAP B11. 3400 Las Vegas Blvd S Ⓦ mirage. com. This resort opened in 2021 and provides not one, but three hotels from different premium Hilton brands: The Hilton, Conrad and, if you're looking to push the boat out, Crockfords. A 5.5-acre pool complex, including an infinity pool weaves between them, as does a plethora of higher-end restaurants and shops. **$$$**

SAHARA MAP P.64, POCKET MAP L4. 2535 Las Vegas Blvd S Ⓦ slslasvegas.com. Originally felling disconnected from the Strip proper, the Sahara has thrived long enough to endure this disconnected spell and newer neighbours mean here may be an uptick for this rare surviving casino from the 50s. **$$**

THE STRAT MAP P.64, POCKET MAP L2. 2000 Las Vegas Blvd S Ⓦ thestrat. com. Much too far to walk to from either the Strip or downtown, the Strat is at least something of a destination in its own right – the rooms aren't in the 1000ft tower, but guests do get free admission. Find the right cut-price offer online, and its simple but sizeable rooms may suit your budget. **$**

TI (TREASURE ISLAND) MAP P.64, POCKET MAP G3. 3300 Las Vegas Blvd S Ⓦ treasureisland.com. Like the building itself, the rooms at TI remain in good condition – they're nothing fancy, but they look reasonably fresh and have good beds – and the location is great too. These days, the whole place, and the pool in particular, attracts a young party crowd. Look out for online discounts. **$$**

THE TROPICANA MAP P.26, POCKET MAP C4. 3801 Las Vegas Blvd S Ⓦ troplv. com. Completely overhauled in 2010, this long-standing landmark can't quite match its Mirage-owned neighbours for dining and nightlife, but is a solid choice for a place to stay. It offers large, cream-and-orange-rooms with new furnishings, an excellent pool complex and a location handy for the airport. **$**

VDARA MAP P.40, POCKET MAP E9. 2600 W Harmon Ave Ⓦ vdara.com. Hedonist holidaymakers might feel ill at ease with the austere steel-and-chrome aesthetic of this CityCenter all-suite hotel, and its lack of a casino, but if you're here to work, or just fancy an escape from Las Vegas's round-the-clock scene, it makes a peaceful and very comfortable retreat. **$$$$**

THE VENETIAN MAP P.64, POCKET MAP G4. 3355 Las Vegas Blvd S Ⓦ venetian. com. In terms of amenities in the property as a whole, and sheer comfort in its guest rooms, The Venetian ranks in the very top tier of Strip hotels; slightly more old-fashioned than Wynn, but still a true pampering experience. All the rooms are suites; you step down from the sleeping area, with its huge bed, to reach a sunken living space near the panoramic windows. Unusually, the price for advance bookings often remains the same for weekends as for weekdays. **$$$$**

WYNN LAS VEGAS MAP P.64, POCKET MAP J2. 3131 Las Vegas Blvd S Ⓦ wynnlasvegas.com. With the arguable exception of the all-but-identical Encore alongside, this is as opulent as it gets in Vegas. The super-large rooms are tastefully decorated and equipped with luxurious linens, and bathrooms feature marble tubs, walk-in showers and even TVs. **$$$$**

Downtown

THE D MAP P.80, POCKET MAP G12. 301 E Fremont St Ⓦ thed.com. Since turning from Fitzgerald's into The D, this central downtown hotel has become a real bargain. All its rooms have had a top-to-bottom makeover (each has two queen beds) and the amenities downstairs are much improved. The one problem can be noise from the Experience outside. **$**

EL CORTEZ MAP P.80, POCKET MAP H12. 600 E Fremont St Ⓦ elcortezhotelcasino. com. Long renowned as Las Vegas's cheapest casino, El Cortez stands a short but, at night, potentially intimidating walk from the heart of Fremont Street. Once there, everything's in good shape, though

Accommodation price codes

Accommodation has been categorized according to the price codes given below. For more details see page 106.

$ = up to $100 a night
$$ = $101-$175
$$$ = $176-$250
$$$$ = above $250

the "Vintage" rooms, reached via the stairs, are no better than faded motel rooms. The "Cabana" suites, across the street, are much more appealing. Online packages for first-time guests offset room rates with free meals and gaming. **$**

FOUR QUEENS MAP P.80, POCKET MAP G12. 202 E Fremont St ⓦ fourqueens. com. There's no real reason to pick this resolutely old-school downtown stalwart over any of its neighbours, though it has at least kept its rooms up to the adequate but unexciting level, say, of a budget national chain. **No resort fee. $**

FREMONT HOTEL MAP P.80, POCKET MAP G12. 200 E Fremont St ⓦ fremontcasino.com. As one of the few downtown casinos owned by a major corporation – Boyd Gaming – the Fremont keeps its standards pretty high. The rooms are small but up to date, with pleasant decor and linens, and it's really not a bad alternative if you fancy being in the thick of the Fremont Street action. **$**

THE GOLDEN GATE MAP P.80, POCKET MAP G11. 1 E Fremont St ⓦ goldengatecasino.com. Las Vegas's first ever hotel, one hundred years old in 2006, has been restyled as a 106-room "boutique hotel", with the promise that more suites will soon be added in a new extension. Yes, the rooms are small and the floors strangely lumpy, but you do get a true taste of Vegas history – plus, unfortunately, a blast of noise from the Experience. **$**

GOLDEN NUGGET MAP P.80, POCKET MAP G12. 129 E Fremont St ⓦ goldennugget.com. Downtown's classiest option is the only hotel hereabouts with amenities – like its amazing pool – to match the Strip giants. The actual rooms, at their freshest but loudest in the Rush Tower overlooking Fremont Street, are smart and comfortable, if not all that exciting. **$**

MAIN STREET STATION MAP P.80, POCKET MAP G11. 200 N Main St ⓦ mainstreetcasino.com. A short but safe walk north of Fremont Street, this large and reasonably modern casino is always good value, for accommodation, food and drink; it's particularly good as an affordable base for a busy weekend. Ask for a room away from the interstate. **$**

THE PLAZA MAP P.80, POCKET MAP F11. 1 Main St ⓦ plazahotelcasino.com. The veteran Plaza, at the end of Fremont Street on the site of Las Vegas's original railroad station, pulled off a real coup in 2011. It bought up the brand-new fixtures and fittings from the prestigious Fontainebleau on the Strip, so badly hit by the recession it never even opened (although it may well be finally open by 2024) and used them to turn its run-down rooms into some of the smartest and best-value lodgings around. **$**

SIN CITY HOSTEL MAP P.80, POCKET MAP F14 1208 Las Vegas Blvd S ⓦ sincityhostel.com. Popular with younger travellers, this basic but clean hostel is located midway between the northern Strip (The Strat) and Downtown, and a few blocks from the upcoming Arts District. The eight-bed female or mixed dorms are bare-bones with an en-suite bathroom and lockers for bags and valuables. There's also comparatively cheap parking here, but space is very limited so reserve a spot well in advance. **$**

The rest of the city

GOLD COAST MAP P.88, POCKET MAP G15. 4000 W Flamingo Rd, ⓦ goldcoastcasino.com. Sedate, old-fashioned local casino, complete with bingo and a bowling alley, a hot half-mile west of the Strip (to which it's connected by free shuttle buses), but right by the fancier Rio and Palms. The rooms are not at all bad, but there's no earthly reason to stay unless the price is right. **$**

ORLEANS MAP P.88, POCKET MAP A12. 4500 W Tropicana Ave ⓦ orleanscasino. com. Provided you get one of its freshly renovated rooms and you have a car to get around, the Orleans, a mile west of the Strip, can serve as an affordable base to explore Las Vegas. The on-site cinema is a real boon. **$$**

THE PALMS MAP P.88, POCKET MAP F16. 4321 W Flamingo Rd Ⓦ palms.com. One of the very few off-Strip casinos that you might genuinely want to stay in, rather than simply find a good-value rate for, the Palms is renowned for its clubs, gigs and weekend buzz. Things are much quieter on weekdays, but with such comfortable rooms and great pools, it can be a real bargain. $$

RIO MAP P.88, POCKET MAP H15. 3700 W Flamingo Rd Ⓦ caesars.com/rio-las-vegas. Part of the Caesars Entertainment empire, but separated by half a mile from its Strip siblings, the Rio really isn't a bad accommodation option. As well as high-class amenities and entertainment, it offers comfortable rooms (large but not suites, as they claim). The Palms is over the road, but you may feel you're missing out on all the action. $

SAM'S TOWN MAP P.88, POCKET MAP D12. 5111 Boulder Hwy Ⓦ samstownlv.com. Quietly prospering from meeting its middle-American customers' needs with Wild West shops, restaurants and bars, this old-fashioned locals casino stands resolutely apart from modern Las Vegas. If you want to dip into town but stay somewhere more peaceful, its comfortable rooms may suit you fine. It's a six-mile shuttle ride to the Strip so you're better off with a car. $$

SUNSET STATION MAP P.88, POCKET MAP D13. 1301 W Sunset Rd, Henderson Ⓦ sunsetstation.com. This huge, attractive and well-equipped casino, ten miles southeast of the Strip en route towards Arizona, would seem impressive anywhere else. Here, despite its pool and fine restaurants, it counts as low-key, and only worth considering if the price is right or you're passing by. $$

VIRGIN HOTELS LAS VEGAS MAP P.88, POCKET MAP A16 4455 Paradise Rd Ⓦ hilton.com. If you know what you're coming for – to mix with partying 20-somethings – the *Virgin Hotels Las Vegas* will suit you perfectly. The rooms are cool and comfortable, and you can even open the floor-to-ceiling windows.

It's too far from the Strip, though, to make a good base for seeing the city as a whole. $$

WESTGATE LAS VEGAS RESORT MAP P.88, POCKET MAP L5. 3000 Paradise Rd Ⓦ westgateresorts.com. How the mighty are fallen. The only reason to stay in the former Hilton – once, as home to Elvis, Las Vegas's premier hotel – is if you're attending a convention next door. Otherwise, the rooms just aren't good enough to compensate for the cut-off location and general air of decay. $$

Mount Charleston

MOUNT CHARLESTON LODGE 5375 Kyle Canyon Rd Ⓦ mtcharlestonlodge.com. An accidental fire destroyed the original lodge in 2021. But now, nineteen comfortably appointed log cabins have opened, alongside the restaurant (see page 103). Lacking phones, wi-fi and TV reception, they're especially popular with honeymooners escaping Las Vegas. $$

RETREAT ON CHARLESTON PEAK 2 Kyle Canyon Rd Ⓦ retreatoncharlestonpeak.com. Set below Hwy-157, facing a towering rocky outcrop 17 miles up from US-95, the best accommodation option in the mountains holds 61 cozy, smart rooms, arranged around an artificial lake. $$.

Grand Canyon South Rim

BRIGHT ANGEL LODGE Grand Canyon South Rim, AZ. Advance reservations Ⓦ grandcanyonlodges.com. Stretching along the South Rim and consisting of a grand lodge flanked by individual cabins, this fantastic option is usually booked up months in advance. Some units share bathrooms, while others enjoy canyon views. $$$

EL TOVAR Grand Canyon South Rim, AZ. Advance reservations Ⓦ grandcanyonlodges.com. At heart an overgrown log cabin, this magnificent, century-old hotel, a symphony in dark wood, is the definitive national park lodge. Although it's very close to the rim, only three of its 78 rooms offer substantial canyon views. Advanced booking necessary. **$$$$**

very attractive, and there's a good pool with hot tubs. **$$$$**

Zion National Park

DESERT PEARL INN 707 Zion Park Blvd, Springdale UT ⓦ desertpearl.com. An absolutely gorgeous hotel, ranged alongside the Virgin River just outside the park, with superb views. From the parking areas it may look like a regular motel, but the actual rooms are huge, modern and

ZION LODGE Zion National Park, UT. Advance reservations, ⓦ zionlodge.com. The only accommodation option inside the national park, occupying pride of place on lush lawns in the heart of the Canyon. The forty en-suite cabins and six suites have gas fireplaces and private porches, while the 76 motel rooms are plainer, but still have porches or balconies. **$$$$**

ESSENTIALS

The interior of the Golden Nugget Casino

Arrival

A very high proportion of visitors to Las Vegas **fly** into the city's only significant airport, not far east of the Strip, while all the rest **drive** across the empty desert from elsewhere in the USA. No passenger trains currently serve the city, though there's talk of constructing a high-speed link with Los Angeles.

By air

Las Vegas's ever-expanding **Harry Reid International Airport** (ⓦ harryreidairport.com) lies immediately southeast of the Strip; aircraft pass within a mile of Mandalay Bay and the Tropicana as they taxi. However, both its terminals – confusingly numbered 1 and 3, since the new Terminal 3, used by all international flights, replaced the former Terminal 2 in 2012 – are accessed from the east, via Paradise Road. That means the closest Strip casinos are around three miles by road from the airport; the Venetian and Wynn more like five miles; and downtown hotels around seven miles.

Assuming you're not renting a car – in which case, note that all the rental companies are based at a separate, off-site facility (see page 118) – much the best way to transfer from the airport to your hotel is by **taxi**. In principle, a cab ride to the southern Strip (10–20min) will cost $24 and upwards, and to the northern Strip (20–30min) more like $35. If the traffic's bad you may have to pay up to $10 more.

Lone travellers may prefer to pay for a seat in a shared **Bell Trans shuttle bus** (ⓦ airportshuttlelasvegas. com), but as these services drop off other passengers en route the journey time can be long, an hour or more for properties on the North Strip. It's often roughly the same price for two people to get a taxi instead.

It is also possible, but even slower, to use the **RTC bus network** (see page 117), by taking route #109 from the airport to the South Strip Transfer Terminal, and changing there onto the Strip And Downtown Express. The journey is likely to take at least half an hour for the South Strip, and over an hour for the North Strip and downtown.

Note that the **Las Vegas Monorail** (see page 118) does not serve the airport.

By car

The main driving route into Las Vegas is the **I-15** interstate, which connects the city with Los Angeles, 270 miles southwest, and Salt Lake City, 420 miles northeast. On Fridays especially, it tends to be clogged with cars arriving from southern California. Only if traffic is at a standstill is it worth leaving the interstate before you reach the exit closest to your final destination. If you're coming from California, therefore, you wouldn't normally expect to drive the full length of Las Vegas Boulevard, which runs parallel to I-15 from the southern end of the valley, and becomes the Strip roughly ten miles along.

Driving to Las Vegas from the Grand Canyon or anywhere else in Arizona, you'll approach the city along **US-93**, via the Hoover Dam. Follow the same road, which turns into Boulder Highway, all the way to downtown, or turn west, most likely on Tropicana Road or Flamingo Avenue, to reach the Strip.

By bus

Long-distance **Greyhound buses** (ⓦ greyhound.com), which connect Las Vegas with other Southwestern cities including Los Angeles, Phoenix and Salt Lake City, stop downtown rather than on the Strip. The station is alongside the Plaza hotel, at 200 S Main Street.

Getting around

If you're visiting Las Vegas specifically to spend time on the Strip and/or downtown – as most visitors do – there's no point renting a car. Downtown is small enough to walk around, while a good **bus service** (the Deuce) runs the length of the Strip and continues to downtown, and there are also several separate **monorail systems** on the Strip. Only if you expect to explore further afield – to outlying areas (see page 86), or to the surrounding desert (see page 96) – does a car become essential.

On foot

It comes as a big surprise to most visitors quite how much **walking** you have to do in Las Vegas. The Strip might look like a simple straight line on the map, but it has a peculiar geography all of its own; the colossal scale of the buildings tricks the eye, making them look smaller and nearer than they really are. Each individual casino can measure a mile end to end, while walking from, say, a restaurant in one property to a club in the next can take half an hour. Especially in summer, when the searing heat makes it all but impossible to walk more than a block or two outdoors, plotting a route from A to B becomes a real art, involving cutting through air-conditioned casinos, catching the occasional monorail and other such dodges.

By bus

While **RTC buses** (ⓦ rtcsnv.com) cover the whole city, two routes meet almost all visitors' needs. Buy tickets before boarding; machines at stops along both routes sell passes for 2 hours, 24 hours, or 3 days. All buses have wheelchair access.

The **Deuce on the Strip** (daily 24hr) runs the full length of the Strip, from Mandalay Bay to the Strat, stopping outside all the casinos, and also loops around downtown, running north on Casino Center Boulevard and south on Las Vegas Boulevard. While its principal downtown stop is where the Fremont Street Experience meets Las Vegas Boulevard, it also stops in both directions at the Bonneville Transit Center (BTC), six blocks south at Bonneville and Casino Center, the main interchange for crosstown routes.

As the name suggests, the faster **Strip & Downtown Express**, or SDX, (daily 9am–midnight) also connects the Strip with downtown, but with fewer stops. In addition, rather than follow the Strip between Wynn Las Vegas and the Strat, it detours west to run past the Convention Center. Downtown, the most useful stop is where the Fremont Street Experience meets Casino Center Boulevard, though the route loops back west beyond Fremont Street to terminate at the Las Vegas Premium Outlets (North) mall, and it also stops at the Bonneville Transit Center. Southbound SDX buses stop on the Strip outside the Fashion Show Mall, Bellagio, Excalibur and Mandalay Bay; northbound buses stop across from Mandalay Bay, and outside the MGM Grand, Paris and Wynn. The southern end of the route is the South Strip Transfer Terminal (SSTT), three miles southeast of Mandalay Bay at 6675 Gilespie Street, which connects with other bus routes and is also served by free airport shuttle buses.

In addition, various free **shuttle buses** connect the Strip with further-flung casinos. From Harrah's, buses run west to the Rio (every 30min, daily 10am–1am) and east to Sam's Town (every 1hr 30min, daily 9.30am–9.30pm). From the intersection of Flamingo Road with the Strip, buses run via the Gold Coast to the Orleans (half-hourly departures, daily 9.30am–12.30am).

By monorail

Four separate monorail systems currently operate along different stretches of the Strip. The longest, but in some respects least useful, is the one officially called the **Las Vegas Monorail** (Mon 7am–midnight, Tues–Thurs 7am–2am, Fri–Sun 7am–3am; ⓦ lvmonorail.com). It runs behind the casinos on the eastern side of the Strip, from the MGM Grand to SLS Las Vegas, detouring east en route to call at the Convention Center. Had the route been extended south to the airport, and downtown in the north, it could have relieved Las Vegas's traffic problems. As it is, it's only conceivably helpful for hops along the southern Strip. Even then, all the stations are located right at the back of the relevant casinos, ten minutes' walk from their Strip entrances, so it can be slower to catch the Monorail than to walk.

All the other three monorail systems are **free**, and link small groups of neighbouring casinos. The southernmost connects Mandalay Bay with Excalibur, via Luxor. The second runs from the Monte Carlo, via Aria and Crystals in CityCenter, to Bellagio; it's a futuristic ride, but be warned that the Bellagio station is in that property's far southwestern corner, far from the casino floor and the Strip. Finally, there's the short link between the Mirage and TI now, which serves little practical function other than keeping pedestrians cool.

By car

Locals might find it hard to believe, but for visitors, **driving** in Las Vegas can be a real pleasure. The thrill of cruising along the Strip, with its sights and sounds and blazing signs, only wears thin if you're actually trying to get somewhere by a certain time. Tourists tend naturally to avoid the worst times for traffic, like the morning rush hour.

Recently, however, the major Strip casinos have broken with tradition by imposing sizeable **parking fees** on all visitors, even their own overnight guests ("resort fees" do not include parking). It's a major disincentive to renting a car. Most downtown casinos charge non-guests for parking, often waived if you use their restaurants or bars.

Car rental is available from almost every Strip or downtown hotel; as a rule each holds one or two outlets of the major rental chains. However, you can find a much wider choice, and usually better rates, if you pick up at the airport. That said, the major rental agencies are no longer based at the airport itself, but at the **Rent-A-Car Center**, three miles southwest at 7135 Gilespie Street, which is connected with the terminals by free shuttle buses. If you're already in the city and decide to rent a car, be sure to take a cab direct to the Rent-A-Car Center.

Campervans can be a comfortable way to move around, particularly if you are driving to the deserts. Campervan North America (ⓦ campervannorthamerica.com) has a branch in Las Vegas at 4324 West Reno Avenue.

By taxi

Since Strip casinos started to charge parking fees, services such as Uber and Lyft have boomed in Las Vegas and are readily available throughout the city. Crucially however, these Uber and Lyft cars are not permitted to stop at the entrances of most casinos and so you'll have to walk some way beyond that to a designated pickup point, usually highlighted on the app.

As for traditional **taxis**, you can't hail one on the street, but long lines of cabs wait at the airport, and at casino entrances. Meters calculate a set starting fare for the first mile and a slightly lower fee for each additional mile, but also continue to run if you're delayed in traffic. There's an additional surcharge for trips to or from the airport (see page 116). Fifteen percent is the usual tip for the driver.

Gambling

Gambling, or as they like to call it these days "**gaming**", lies at the root of everything in Las Vegas. Only one visitor in ten doesn't gamble at all; the rest lose an average of $500 each in the casinos. Whether you're pumping coins into a slot machine or trying to beat the dealer at blackjack, the rules always mean the casino enjoys the "house edge". So long as you're 21 or over, and carrying ID to prove it, you can gamble anywhere you like. The glamour of the large **Strip casinos** can be seductive, but the minimum stake for each game tends to be higher, and the odds a little worse. Many visitors prefer to gamble **downtown**, where the atmosphere is a bit more down-and-dirty and their money holds out longer. Either way, decide in advance how much you're prepared to lose, and stop if you reach that point.

In all casinos waitresses will ply you with free drinks as long as you are gambling; tips are expected. If you gamble for any length of time, join the casino's free players club; it can earn you meals, freebies and future stays.

Baccarat

Formerly the preserve of high-rolling "whales", **baccarat** (pronounced bah-kah-rah) accounts for over forty percent of the casinos' revenue from table games. Played with an ordinary pack in which each numbered card counts its face value (aces are 1 not 11), except tens, jacks, queens and kings, all valued at zero, it's a simple game of luck. Only two hands are dealt, the "player" and the "bank". Each aims to reach a total value of nine; you can bet on either, but the bank has a slightly better chance of winning. The house advantage comes because the casino rakes off a small commission.

Blackjack

Also known as "21" or "pontoon", **blackjack** remains Las Vegas's favourite card game. Players compete against the bank, attempting to build a hand that adds nearly, or exactly, to 21. Tens, jacks, queens and kings count as ten points, aces as either one or eleven. Players make their bets before receiving two cards, then each in turn plays their hand through to completion, saying "hit" to receive additional cards, and either "stand" to stop, or "bust" if the total exceeds 21. The dealer plays last, according to fixed rules that preclude individual judgement. The house advantage comes because players who go bust lose their stakes whether or not the dealer does too. Players can minimize that advantage by learning the "correct" response to every situation – it's so hard that some casinos happily provide gamblers with the relevant charts.

Craps

If you don't know how to play the dice game **craps**, played on a high-walled baize table, take a lesson (freely available in most casinos)

– you'll never be able to learn it from watching. The basic idea is that a different "shooter" throws a pair of dice each time around. Players bet on either "pass" or "don't pass" before the first throw, known as the "come-out roll". If that throw is 7 or 11, "pass" has won; if it's 2, 3 or 12, "don't pass" wins. Anything else, and the shooter throws again, and keeps doing so until either matching the original throw – a win for "pass" – or throwing 7 – a win for "don't pass". All sorts of side bets capture the imaginations of serious gamblers.

Poker

In **poker**, players compete against each other, not the house, to build the best five-card hand (see page 120). The two most popular variations are Seven Card Stud, in which each player receives two cards face down, four face up, and then the last face down, and Texas Hold 'Em, in which your two face-down cards are supplemented by five face-up communal cards. The casino rakes off a percentage of each pot. You're therefore playing against whoever else happens to be around; it's possible to win, but it's a big risk to assume you're the best player at the table.

Casinos also offer what's effectively poker played in a **blackjack format**, in which each player attempts to beat the dealer. Formats include Let It Ride, Pai Gow Poker and Caribbean Stud.

Roulette

Roulette is the game in which a ball lands in a numbered slot in a rotating wheel. You can bet on the specific number, or group of numbers, and if the slot is "red" or "black". Winners are paid as though the wheel holds 36 slots, but it usually holds 38, thanks to two green slots, 0 and 00. Always look for wheels that hold only one zero slot, and thus offer better odds. You can't get your money back by repeatedly redoubling your stake; tables only allow bets up to a quickly reached maximum.

Slot machines

Casinos make more money from **slot machines** than from anything else. All machines are programmed to pay out a percentage of their intake as winnings. On average, visitors feed $1600 per day into every single machine in the city, and win $1500 back again, leaving the casino $100 profit. The slots downtown offer better odds than on the Strip.

A "non-progressive" machine always pays the same for a specific winning combination and pays smaller but more frequent jackpots. "Progressive" slots, such as Wheel of Fortune, are linked into networks where the overall jackpot can climb into millions of dollars, before someone scoops the lot.

Video poker is an addictive cross between traditional slot machines and the table game. The odds can be so

Ranking of poker hands

Straight flush Five consecutive cards in the same suit.
Four of a kind Four aces, four sevens, etc.
Full house Three of a kind and a separate pair.
Flush Any five cards in the same suit.
Straight Five consecutive cards not in the same suit.
Three of a kind Three kings, three sixes, etc.
Two pair Two fours and two jacks, etc.
One pair Two tens, etc.

good that on certain machines, players who play a perfect strategy have a slight advantage over the house.

Sports betting

Las Vegas is all but unique in the USA in offering visitors the chance to bet on sports events legally, in the highly charged atmosphere of a major casino. Almost every casino has either a **Sports Book**, or if it covers horseracing as well, a Race and Sports Book, which vary from comfortable high-tech lounges to something more like a raucous neighbourhood sports bar. All offer much the same odds on any specific event and many offer "in-running" wagering, meaning moment-by-moment bets on games currently in progress.

Directory A–Z

Accessible Travel

The **Las Vegas Convention and Visitors Authority** offers detailed advice for disabled visitors; download the Access Las Vegas brochure from ⓦ lasvegas.com, or call their advice line on ☏ 702 892 0711.

All the casinos in Las Vegas are **wheelchair accessible** and offer hotel rooms designed to suit visitors with disabilities. Don't underestimate the sheer scale of each casino, let alone the Strip as a whole; an individual destination like a restaurant or a theatre may be a long way from the nearest parking space. If you need to rent specific mobility equipment, contact Ability Center, 6001 S Decatur Blvd (☏ 702 434 3030, ⓦ abilitycenter. com). For public transport, both Bell Trans shuttle buses from the airport (☏ 800 274 7433, ⓦ airportshuttlelas vegas.com) and RTC buses in the city itself (ⓦ rtcsnv.com) are wheelchair accessible.

If you plan to drive yourself, note that the national rental chains offer adapted vehicles, and visitors can arrange temporary free **disabled parking permits** via the Nevada Department of Motor Vehicles (☏ 775 684 4750 or ☏ 702 486 4368, ⓦ dmv. nv.com).

Cinemas

Typical ticket prices for cinemas in Las Vegas are around $10 for matinee performances, starting before 6pm, and $15 for evening shows.
AMC Town Square 18 Town Square, 6587 Las Vegas Blvd S ⓦ amctheatres. com.
Brenden Theatres & IMAX The Palms, 4321 W Flamingo Rd ⓦ brendentheatres.com.
Century 18 Orleans, 4500 W Tropicana Ave ⓦ cinemark.com.
Century 18 Sam's Town, 5111 Boulder Hwy ⓦ cinemark.com.
Regal 13 Sunset Station, 1301 W Sunset Rd, Henderson ⓦ regmovies. com.
There is no cinema on the Strip.

Crime

While you're safe in the major public spaces of Las Vegas, such as inside the security-conscious casinos, crime can be a problem elsewhere. Away from the crowded Strip, which has its own problems with **pickpockets** and bag-snatchers, you can feel exposed and

Emergency numbers

In any medical or security emergency, call ☏ 911.

Eating out price codes

Throughout this guide, restaurants have been categorized as per the below, based on a two-course meal for one with a soft drink.

$ = up to $30
$$ = $31-$50
$$$ = $51-$100
$$$$ = Above $100

vulnerable if you walk any distance outdoors. It's essential to keep your cash hidden at all times, not to flaunt valuables like cameras and iPads, and not to tell strangers your hotel room number. Be cautious in multistorey parking garages, especially at night, and try to park close to the exits. In times when mass shootings can happen anywhere in the US, be aware of any suspicious situations.

Electricity

The **electricity** supply in Las Vegas, as in all of the USA, is 110 volts AC, and uses two-pin plugs. Bring or buy an adapter, and if necessary a voltage converter as well, if you're travelling from a country that uses a different system and need to use your own electrical appliances.

Health

In any medical emergency, call ☎ 911. The front desk or phone operator at your hotel will be able to advise on sources of appropriate help. **Hospitals** that have 24hr emergency rooms include Sunrise Hospital, 3186 S Maryland Parkway (ⓦ sunrisehospital. com), and the University Medical Center, 1800 W Charleston Blvd (ⓦ umcsn.com). For more minor issues, head to the Harmon Medical Center, 150 E Harmon Ave (Mon–Fri 8am–8pm, ⓦ elitelv.com).

Twenty-four-hour **pharmacies** on the Strip include the CVS Pharmacy, alongside the Monte Carlo at 3758 Las Vegas Blvd S (☎ 702 262 9028) and Walgreens, beside the main Palazzo

entrance at 3339 Las Vegas Blvd S (☎ 702 369 8166).

To find a local **dentist**, contact the Nevada Dental Association (☎ 702 255 4211, ⓦ nvda.org).

Internet

Every casino/hotel in Las Vegas provides in-room **wi-fi** access for its guests, and more often than not, it is free. In almost all cases, internet access forms the largest component of the compulsory "resort fee" (see page 107), which typically costs at least $20 per day, and may well cover one device only; elsewhere, hotel guests can generally choose to pay a stand-alone fee. On top of that, if you're spending time in a casino other than one you're staying in, you won't normally have wi-fi access.

Several casinos, however, including most of the MGM Resorts properties, offer **free wi-fi** access to everyone in their public areas, as opposed to the guest rooms. In addition, a handful of shops and cafés along the Strip provide free wi-fi to customers (and anyone who happens to be in the immediate vicinity): *Coffee Bean & Tea Leaf* in Planet Hollywood's Miracle Mile (see page 56); and the Apple Store and *Starbucks* in the Fashion Show Mall (see page 70).

Free wi-fi is also available throughout McCarran International Airport.

Las Vegas Power Pass

Las Vegas Power Pass (ⓦ lasvegas pass.com) is the sightseeing card which gives holders entry to over 50 top Vegas attractions, bus tours and museums. The pass is available for 1 day, 2 days, 3 days or 5 days.

LGBTQ+ travellers

Las Vegas welcomes **LGBTQ+ travellers** with open arms. Several resorts host specifical LGBTQ+ events, such as pool parties branded Temptation Sundays at Luxor, and the Elevate PRIDE Pool Party at Sahara. Top-of-their-game drag performers take to the stage each weekend at The Garden Las Vegas' Bottomless Drag Brunch, while Charlie's features entertainment like drag and karaoke.

For those not in the market for a wild night, the Fun Hog Ranch frequently partners with the LGBTQ+ comunity to run themed events, while The Garage provides laid-back patio seating, so you can soak up the Nevada sun.

Historically, the city's gay-oriented nightlife focuses around what's fondly known as the "**Fruit Loop**", a mile east of the Strip, where Paradise Road, running south from the Hard Rock, meets Naples Drive. Well-known clubs in the neighbourhood include Piranha (see page 95), but there are none exclusively geared towards women.

The best source of information on current issues and events in Las Vegas's gay community are ⓦgaylasvegas.com, ⓦgogaynevada.com or ⓦlasvegaspride.org.

Since same-sex marriage was declared legal in Nevada in 2014, the major casino chapels have rushed to offer gay wedding ceremonies, even if certain private chapels have refused. The **Viva Las Vegas Wedding Chapel**, 1205 Las Vegas Blvd S (ⓦgaychapeloflasvegas.com) offers a full range of ceremonies; Elvis is optional.

The annual **Las Vegas Pride** event, celebrated in late October (ⓦlasvegaspride.org), kicks off with a Friday night parade through downtown, while the Saturday sees an open-air festival in Sunset Park, at the corner of Sunset Road and Eastern Avenue, 10 miles south of downtown.

In May, the **Nevada Gay Rodeo Association** (ⓦngra.com) holds the three-day BigHorn Rodeo at Horseman's Park, 5800 E Flamingo Rd.

Money

Las Vegas is not a budget destination in any meaningful sense. The days are gone when casinos used cut-price food and entertainment to lure in gamblers. Now everything from restaurants to showrooms have to make a profit, and prices are high. A typical all-you-can-eat buffet costs $30 or more for dinner; a run-of-the-mill restaurant more like $60 per head, without drinks; and a gourmet place double that or

---

Public holidays

Jan 1 New Year's Day
Jan 15 Martin Luther King Jr's Birthday
3rd Mon in Feb Presidents' Day
Last Mon in May Memorial Day
July 4 Independence Day
1st Mon in Sept Labor Day
2nd Mon in Oct Columbus Day
Nov 11 Veterans' Day
Last Thurs in Nov Thanksgiving Day
Dec 25 Christmas Day

more. There are plenty of fast food chains for cheaper eats.

Tickets for a show can easily cost $100 or more, while a night out in a big club is liable to cost hundreds, and potentially thousands, of dollars.

Hotel room rates are generally good value, and on weekdays compare favourably with what you'd get for the same money elsewhere in the USA, but can run into hundreds per night on weekends. On top of that, of course, the average visitor also loses several hundred dollars gambling.

As for how you bring your money, it's assumed everywhere that you'll use a **credit card** for all significant expenses. It's extremely easy to get cash anywhere on the Strip; ATMs are everywhere, though all tend to charge for withdrawals.

Travellers from overseas are advised not to bring foreign cash; there are no banks on the Strip, and while the casinos will gladly change your cash you won't get a good rate.

Phones

Foreign visitors can assume that their **mobile phones** (cell phones) will work in Las Vegas, though it's worth checking with your phone provider that your existing payment scheme will cover you there, and what the call charges are. Many providers offer short-term pricing packages designed to make holiday phone usage more affordable. If you plan to access the internet using your phone, make sure that you know your provider's roaming charges, which may well be extremely expensive.

For all calls, you can make tremendous savings by using **Skype**, or similar programmes, to make free wi-fi calls from your phone or laptop. Alternatively, prepaid **phone cards** are widely available from casino convenience stores, petrol (gas) stations, supermarkets and other outlets. Many casinos, especially those

that charge resort fees (see page 107), offer guests free local phone calls; making an international call from your hotel room phone is always liable to be very expensive.

Smoking

Smoking remains legal in the public areas of all casinos, and in bars that do not serve food. It is forbidden in restaurants, including those inside casinos, though smoke does waft into those restaurants that are open to the casino floor. All hotels offer non-smoking rooms.

Tax

Sales tax of 8.25 percent is charged on all purchases in Las Vegas. Hotel rates are subject to an additional **room tax** of twelve percent on the Strip, and thirteen percent downtown (see page 107).

Time

Las Vegas is in the **Pacific Time Zone**, three hours behind the Eastern Time Zone. It's almost always eight hours behind the UK, though clocks in the US move forward by one hour on the second Sunday in March and back one hour on the first Sunday in November, placing them briefly out of synch with clocks in the UK.

Tipping

Tipping etiquette can often seem complicated and frustrating to visitors unused to it, because it is. If you find yourself wondering whether to tip, do. Servers in restaurants depend on tips for their income and expect at least fifteen percent. So do cab drivers. If someone carries your bags, tip $1–2 per bag; valet parking attendants expect $2; and it's usual to leave a tip of $1 or $2 per day when you leave your hotel room. When gambling, it's considered appropriate to tip the dealer a chip or two if you win. Bar staff, or casino waitresses bringing free drinks, expect $1–2 per drink. Increasingly, fast food restaurants and shops such as Walgreens ask you to add an optional tip at the payment counter.

Tourist information

The best single source of information on the city is ⓦ lasvegas.com, the website of the **Las Vegas Convention and Visitor Authority** (LVCVA). They also run a visitor centre at 3150 Paradise Rd, half a mile east of the Strip (Mon–Fri 8am–5pm), but it offers nothing you can't find much more easily elsewhere.

Other useful websites include:
ⓦ **dmckee.lvablog.com** The "Stiffs and Georges" blog is a lively but serious source of news and comment on Las Vegas and the casino industry.
ⓦ **eatinglv.com** This long-running blog holds a huge archive of restaurant reviews.
ⓦ **lasvegassun.com** Las Vegas's best daily newspaper website.
ⓦ **lasvegasweekly.com** A good source of current listings, plus a handy archive of their annual "Best of Las Vegas" awards in all sorts of categories.
ⓦ **spotlight.vegas** Schedules and deals for concerts and shows; a good place to find out what's happening while you're in town.

Tours

Las Vegas does not offer the kind of **sightseeing tours** familiar in other cities. Almost everything of interest in the city itself is in and around the casinos; you can't really appreciate them from a passing bus, and they're too big to explore more than one or two at a time on foot. **Bus tours** do, however, head further afield. Thus Gray Line (ⓦ graylinelasvegas. com) offers tours to the Hoover Dam (4hr 30min); the Grand Canyon West Rim (11hr); and the Grand Canyon South Rim (14hr). You can also get lucky and buy these tours for much less. Helicopter operators, including Maverick (ⓦ maverickhelicopter.com) and Sundance (ⓦ sundancehelicopters. com), offer brief day or night **"flightseeing" tours** over the Strip, lasting less than fifteen minutes. They and other companies also fly day-trippers east to the Grand Canyon (see page 101).

For something totally different with an extra shot of adrenaline, try RZR Zero 1 Tours. They provide access to Nevada's diverse terrain and new trails by putting you behind the wheel of a high-performance dune buggy (ⓦ zero1offroad.com), at 6975 Speedway Blvd.

Travelling with children

In the early 1990s, Las Vegas flirted briefly with the idea that it might become a child-friendly destination to match Orlando, Florida. That dream was swiftly abandoned; gambling and kids don't make a good mix. Even so, many visitors bring their **kids** to the city; the Strip sidewalk is thronged until after midnight with parents pushing cumbersome buggies and struggling with exhausted children.

There's still a lot about Las Vegas that will appeal to kids, from the castles and pyramids, volcanoes and fountains on the Strip, to more specific paying attractions. Among the most popular with children are the Secret Garden and Dolphin Habitat at the Mirage; Shark Reef at Mandalay Bay; the Bodies and Titanic exhibitions at Luxor; The Hunger Games: The Exhibition at MGM Grand; the gondolas at the Venetian; and the roller coasters and thrill rides at New York–New York, Circus Circus and the Strat.

All the casinos welcome children as guests. Strictly speaking, **under-21s** are not allowed in gambling areas, which means that family groups have to keep walking rather than linger on the casino floor. Casinos do not offer babysitting services, but can provide details of babysitting agencies.

Note that in many casinos, some or all of the swimming pools now operate as adults-only "dayclubs", with drinking, dancing and partying; it's worth checking in advance before you go ahead and book your accommodation.

Weddings

Thanks to Nevada's notoriously minimal legal requirements, and especially the lack of an obligatory waiting period, around 120,000 people get married in Las Vegas each year.

At its simplest, arranging a Vegas wedding is very straightforward. First of all, you need a **Nevada marriage licence**. To get that, both parties must appear in person at the Clark County Marriage License Bureau, 200 South Third St (Mon –Thurs 8am–midnight, Fri–Sun 12pm–midnight; Ⓦclarkcountynv.gov). So long as both are aged 18 or over, not married already and can show picture ID, they'll sell you a licence. Note that there isn't an office on the Strip.

If you've made an advance reservation, you can then walk with your licence to the office of the **Commissioner of Civil Marriages**, on the sixth floor at 330 S Third St (Mon–Thurs 2–6pm, Fri 9.30am–8.45pm, Sat 12.30–8.45pm, Sun 9am–5pm; Ⓦclarkcountynv.gov) and pay a further fee to have the actual ceremony performed. One witness is required; ideally you should bring your own, though what the Commissioner charmingly calls "unsavoury individuals" lurk outside the offices, hoping to sell their services as witnesses.

Just because it's possible to have a quick, cheap wedding in Las Vegas, however, doesn't mean that's what most couples actually do. Instead, most marriages are bespoke celebrations in wedding chapels. These are usually stand-alone structures of the kind reviewed throughout this book, or they can be yet another component in the huge casino-hotels. You can find full listings of chapels and wedding planners on the official Las Vegas CVB website, Ⓦlasvegas.com, and also on the casinos' own websites.

Prices at **wedding chapels** range upwards from around $290 all-in for a bare-bones ceremony. For the full works, which in Las Vegas can include helicopter flights to the Grand Canyon or pretty much anything else you care to mention, the bill can of course run into thousands of dollars. The biggest hidden expense is likely to be photography; be sure to check whether you or your guests will be allowed to bring cameras, and if not, how much the official photos or footage will cost.

Finally, note that now **gay marriage** has become legal in Nevada all the major casino chapels, and most but not all of the private chapels, are happy to perform gay weddings. For more details, see page 123.

Festivals and events

In comparison to most other American cities, Las Vegas does not have an extensive calendar of annual events. In terms of attracting crowds, the biggest events tend to be the opening of new casinos and, even more exciting, the implosions of old ones (see page 65).

NASCAR Weekend

Early March Ⓦlvms.com

Conventions and trade shows

When planning a visit, it's useful to know when the city's biggest **conventions** are happening as room rates can soar.

Mid-Jan Consumer Electronics Show
Mid-Feb Men's Apparel Guild (MAGIC) convention
Mid-April National Association of Broadcasters convention
Mid-Aug Men's Apparel Guild (MAGIC) convention (again)
Early Nov Specialty Equipment Manufacturers Association (SEMA) convention

Three days of racing at the Las Vegas Motor Speedway, 7000 Las Vegas Blvd N at Speedway Blvd.

St Patrick's Day

March 17
Pubs, clubs, casinos and restaurants all celebrate St Patrick's Day.

World Series of Poker

Late May to mid-July
Ⓦ poker.wsop.com
The world's premier poker tournament has been held at the Rio since 1995.

Las Vegas Helldorado Days

Mid-May Ⓦ lasvegasnevada.gov

Five nights of pro rodeo action in Symphony Park – at 100 S Grand Central Parkway, alongside downtown's Smith Center – plus a Saturday night parade downtown.

National Finals Rodeo

Early Dec Ⓦ nfrexperience.com
Ten-day pro rodeo event known as the Super Bowl of Rodeo, held at the Thomas & Mack Center, 4505 S Maryland Parkway.

New Year's Eve

December 31
The biggest night in the city's calendar, marked by concerts and festivities.

Chronology

1598 Spain claims what's now southern Nevada as part of the colony of New Mexico.

1829 Mexican explorers name an unexpected oasis of grasslands "Las Vegas" – "The Meadows".

1847 USA acquires New Mexico.

1864 Nevada becomes a state.

1905 The railroad arrives. Las Vegas is established on May 15, when forty newly drawn blocks are auctioned.

1909 Nevada becomes the first US state to outlaw gambling.

1931 Nevada marks the end of Prohibition by legalizing gambling – the only state to do so.

1935 Hoover Dam, the highest dam in the world, is completed. Las Vegas hosts first convention.

1938 Guy McAfee, former chief of LA's vice squad, takes over the Pair-O-Dice Club, on what he dubs "The Strip".

1940 Las Vegas's population reaches eight thousand.

1941 El Rancho opens as the Strip's first fully fledged resort.

1946 Mobster "Bugsy" Siegel opens the Flamingo; he's murdered six months later after heavy losses.

1950s An unstoppable flow of new Strip resorts includes the Desert Inn, the Sands, the Riviera, the Dunes and the Hacienda. Desert A-bomb tests can be seen and heard from the city.

1966 Caesars Palace, the first themed casino, opens. Howard Hughes is asked to leave the Desert Inn because he isn't gambling; instead, he buys it, along with the Sands, the Silver Slipper and the New Frontier, marking the end of Mob domination.

1969 Kirk Kerkorian opens the world's largest hotel – the Las Vegas Hilton – which hosts Elvis's rebirth as a karate-kicking lounge lizard.

1973 Kirk Kerkorian again opens the world's largest hotel – the original MGM Grand, now Bally's. Steve Wynn takes over downtown's Golden Nugget.

1983 Following disastrous fires at the MGM Grand and the Hilton, Las Vegas seems about to be eclipsed by Atlantic City; direct flights between New York and Las Vegas are discontinued.

1989 Steve Wynn opens the opulent Mirage, complete with volcano. Benny Binion dies, with his Horseshoe downtown still Las Vegas's most profitable casino.

1993 In a short-lived bid to reinvent Las Vegas as a child-friendly destination, Luxor, Treasure Island and the new MGM Grand all open.

1995 Downtown roofed over to create Fremont Street Experience.

1997 New York–New York opens; in a craze for building replica cities, it's followed by Bellagio in 1998 and the Venetian and Paris in 1999.

2005 Harrah's buys Caesars Entertainment, leaving the Strip largely owned by two huge corporations. Wynn Las Vegas opens.

2009 Despite recession, MGM Mirage completes CityCenter.

2011 Carolyn Goodman succeeds her husband Oscar as mayor.

2016 Venetian owner Sheldon Adelson is major donor to Donald Trump's presidential campaign.

2017 A gunman opens fire at a crowd of concert-goers on the Strip, killing 58 and injuring more than 500 people.

2020 The Strip stands empty during Covid 19 lockdown. In June, it's announced Nevada counties and cities will split $148.5 million of grants to aid recovery.

2021 Venetian owner Sheldon Adelson dies. His properties are sold on.

2023 End of an era for the Mirage and its volcano as the Hard Rock International plans its new hotel shaped like a guitar. Meanwhile, it's the start of a new era for the North Strip with more casinos opening.

Publishing Information
Fifth edition 2023

Distribution
UK, Ireland and Europe
Apa Publications (UK) Ltd; sales@roughguides.com
United States and Canada
Ingram Publisher Services; ips@ingramcontent.com
Australia and New Zealand
Booktopia; retailer@booktopia.com.au
Worldwide
Apa Publications (UK) Ltd; sales@roughguides.com

Special Sales, Content Licensing and CoPublishing
Rough Guides can be purchased in bulk quantities at discounted prices. We can
create special editions, personalised jackets and corporate imprints tailored to
your needs. sales@roughguides.com.
roughguides.com

Printed in China

This book was produced using **Typefi** automated publishing software.

A catalogue record for this book is available from the British Library

The publishers and authors have done their best to ensure the accuracy and
currency of all the information in **Pocket Rough Guide Las Vegas**, however, they
can accept no responsibility for any loss, injury, or inconvenience sustained by
any traveller as a result of information or advice contained in the guide.

Rough Guide Credits
Editor: Siobhan Warwicker
Cartography: Katie Bennett
Picture editor: Tom Smyth
Layout: Pradeep Thapliyal
Original design: Richard Czapnik
Head of DTP and Pre-Press:
Rebeka Davies
Head of Publishing: Sarah Clark

About the updater

Paul Stafford is based in Birmingham, UK, but can usually be found anywhere that is not at all like Birmingham. Having lived in five countries across three continents, he has learned a thing or two about quickly getting to grips with unfamiliar places. When not entangled in a web of words and pictures, he is making and releasing music as one half of the rock duo Phwoar.

Find Paul on Twitter and Instagram @paulrstafford.

Acknowledgements

Thanks to Harry Brockhurst at Hills Balfour for keeping me in the loop of the Vegas changes before they even happen (that's no mean feat in the ever-changing maelstrom of Vegas). My special thanks goes to Helena for being the best travel partner and a person to whom the principle of 'the house always wins' seems not to apply.

Help us update

We've gone to a lot of effort to ensure that this edition of the **Pocket Rough Guide Las Vegas** is accurate and up-to-date. However, things change – places get "discovered", opening hours are notoriously fickle, restaurants and rooms raise prices or lower standards. If you feel we've got it wrong or left something out, we'd like to know, and if you can remember the address, the price, the hours, the phone number, so much the better.

Please send your comments with the subject line "**Pocket Rough Guide Las Vegas Update**" to mail@uk.roughguides.com. We'll credit all contributions and send a copy of the next edition (or any other Rough Guide if you prefer) for the very best emails.

Photo Credits

(Key: T-top; C-centre; B-bottom; L-left; R-right)

Al Powers 18B
Denise Truscello/Caesars Entertainment 51, 61
Erik Kabik 60
iStock 6, 77, 85
MGM Resorts International 12/13B, 14T, 16B, 17T, 19B, 33, 37, 104/105
Resorts World Las Vegas 76
Shutterstock 1, 2T, 2BL, 2C, 2BR, 4, 10, 11T, 11B, 12/13T, 12B, 13C, 15B, 15T, 16T, 17B, 18T, 18C, 19T, 19C, 20T, 20C, 20B, 21T, 21C, 21B, 22/23, 25, 29, 30, 31, 38, 39, 41, 42, 45, 49, 53, 55, 56, 59, 63, 71, 75, 79, 81, 86, 87, 93, 97, 98, 100, 102, 103, 114/115
The Boulevard 91
Tim Draper/Rough Guides 14B, 27, 35, 46, 54, 66, 68, 73, 82, 83, 84, 89, 94, 95

Cover: The Golden Nugget and Plaza Hotel and Casino **Kit Leong/Shutterstock**

Index

NOTES